CONFESSIONS
OF A

FORMER

FOX
NEWS
Christian

SETH ANDREWS

outskirts
press

Outskirts Press, Inc.
http://www.outskirtspress.com

PB ISBN: 978-1-9772-2979-3
HB ISBN: 978-1-9772-2486-6

This book is available in audiobook format—
read by the author—at **Audible.com**

Chapter List

We must especially beware of that small group of selfish men who would clip the wings of the American Eagle in order to feather their own nests.

President Franklin Delano Roosevelt
State of the Union, January 6, 1941

Introduction

...

"WHAT'S THIS COUNTRY COMING TO?"

This lament is often heard in Oklahoma, the white-bread, corn-fed, hand-over-heartland red state from which I hail. The question often accompanies misty-eyed nostalgia about what was, what is, and what might have been. It's a frowning rebuke of those godless, treasonous, America-hating, so-called progressives who somehow—despite their giddy obsession with abortion and condoms—have procreated themselves into a real threat to God-and-Country Conservatism.

Liberals are the pockmarks on Lady Liberty's once-pristine countenance. *They must be stopped!*

Only a few short years ago I thought like that. I spoke like that. I lived like that. Had a neurosurgeon dissected my anterior cingulate cortex, he likely would have found a gooey red-white-and-blue tumor created by AM radio frequencies blasting the rants of Rush Limbaugh, Michael Savage, Sean Hannity, Laura Ingraham, and Glenn Beck. Every broadcast provided a fresh opportunity for outrage, most of those (suspiciously white and wealthy) hosts shrieking indignation for three hours every weekday as their (suspiciously white and middle-class) listeners angrily clawed the steering wheels of their (suspiciously foreign) cars.

'Murica was under attack, dammit, and it was the sworn duty of every God-fearing, flag-waving, true-blue patriot to rise up and defend her honor.

Yet outside of some watercooler blather between my Republican buddies and me, the only thing rising was my blood pressure. I voted only in the presidential election, and only along straight party lines. I participated in just one conservative political rally, and by "participated" I mean that I stood in a parking lot with a homemade sign and occasionally yelled "YEAH!" at conservative politicians. I knew little about my local government, my state government, or my federal government, and what I did know about the two major political parties was spoon-fed to me by the frothing daytime talkers and a single television network: Fox News.

Fox News spoke to me. Its flash and patriotic set designs. Its smooth and sexy hosts (well, many of them). Its rapid-fire delivery of affirming, heartland-friendly stories that passionately stroked my Republican skin like it was William F. Buckley's cat. I was a prime-time Fox News addict, daily fueling my righteous discontent about the liberal assault on this great nation, convinced that CNN and the big three networks—ABC, CBS, and NBC—were all in league with each other (and the devil himself) to replace this country with some kind of liberal New World Order.

With Fox News, there was finally a network for the rugged individualist, the staunch capitalist, the Second Amendment warrior, the God defender, the common man.

Founded in 1996 by Australian billionaire Rupert Murdoch and run for twenty years by former Republican media consultant and television exec Roger Aisles, Fox News has blossomed into a ratings behemoth, the fifth-most watched network in prime time (in all of television) and consistently ranking number one among cable news outlets.[1] It's also a major money maker; Fox Corp. earnings topped $2.5 billion in 2019.[2]

Fox News is a media bullet train, its popularity and ratings dominance used as a shield against its critics ("Hey, they're kicking ass, so they're obviously doing something right"). Criticisms yet remain, the network long prompting a palpable disdain among many progressives who protest that the whole damn channel constantly explodes in your face like a Republican Party convention balloon. As such, liberals sometimes snicker about Fake Noise and Fuck News.

But back in the day, I was hooked. Straight out of the gate, Fox News versus CNN felt like a holy war, and as I was the product of a hugely conservative, fundamentalist Christian, rah-rah-Ronald-Reagan culture, I often parroted notions of the "mainstream media," blissfully unaware of the irony that Fox News's ratings dominance and crazy cash flow made it more mainstream than many of its competitors combined. Somehow, even from its glitzy mansion on Murdoch Mountain, Fox News was considered the rogue, the rebel, the Robin Hood, the David to CNN's Goliath.

Other networks were off-kilter. Fox News proudly announced itself with the trademarked slogan "Fair & Balanced," a not-so-subtle indictment of American television journalism.

Fox News's blue-chip players have become brands of their own, and with a few suspiciously—dare I say it—fair exceptions like (the recently departed) Shepherd Smith, Chris Wallace, and others, Fox News has remained doggedly right, so much so that New York Mayor Bill de Blasio blamed the network for the stunning 2016 presidential victory of Donald Trump.[3]

1   Ad Week "2016 Ratings: Fox News Channel is Cable TV's Most-Watched Network" December 28, 2016
2   Broadcasting + Cable "Fox Reports Lower Fourth-Quarter Net" August 7, 2019
3   Politico "De Blasio: Fox News Paved Way for Trump" February 3, 2017

The implication is staggering. A single network pushed its weight, and its legions of viewers tipped the scale. Years ago, I might have proudly tipped along with them.

I'm fascinated by the younger portrait of myself, the conservative couch Christian who baptized himself in a sea of outrage, lamenting the decline of western civilization at the hands of the liberal, the progressive, the permissive, the secular, and the godless. I couldn't yet know that I would one day reject the religious teachings of my youth to stand among the heathens.

The fear of godlessness is deeply embedded in American culture. Even a quick Dictionary.com search for the definition of *godless* reveals the description of a person 1) having or acknowledging no god or deity; atheistic 2) wicked; evil; sinful. How can one be a good American if he/she is wicked, evil, and sinful?

A January 2017 Pew Research survey revealed that 32 percent of Americans believed a true American must first be Christian. Among white evangelical protestants, that number almost doubles (57 percent).[4] As Yahweh owns the earth (Psalm 24:1), the land (Leviticus 25:23), the gold and silver (Haggai 2:8), and all of humanity (1 Corinthians 6:19-20), and as biblical law trumps any of that pesky state/church language in the Establishment Clause of the First Amendment, the faithful gladly proclaim God's dominion over America with absolutely no sense of irony about religious privilege in a representative republic. (They're the privileged; why would they consider it a problem?)

This "majority rule" attitude feeds on itself. With most American citizens identifying with some flavor of Christianity, mob rule quickly takes over. A nation with Christians becomes a Christian Nation, and the secular framework of the United States almost collapses beneath the weight of the steeples and crosses, the soapboxes of

---

4   Pew Research Center "Faith: Few Strong Links to National Identity" February 1, 2017

preacher-politicians, and the avalanche of ratings-porn outrage that splashes down daily from Fox News headquarters.

How had I bought into the notion of a star-spangled theocracy? How had I once been a Fox News Christian? The answer is simple. From my earliest memories, Christian conservativism was my second language, taught and reinforced by my parents, siblings, friends, teachers, guardians, books, toys, music, shows, films, and Sunday sermons.

My mother and father were fundamentalists. Bible scholars. Theologians. They met at Oral Roberts University. My mother wrote a Greek New Testament study guide and teaches New Testament Greek even today. My childhood stories were Bible stories. My Sunday activities were church activities. My school lessons were religious lessons. My parents were hard-core, religious-right conservatives, and they did everything in their power to ensure that their offspring would one day wave the family standard.

Republicans. For God and Country.

I spent the fourth grade in an ultraconservative isolation chamber called Temple Christian, a tiny, church-owned, private school in Tulsa, Oklahoma. (I wrote about TCS in my 2012 autobiography, *Deconverted*, but it warrants mentioning again here.) Temple Christian didn't just teach a Christian Nation narrative. It dressed every student in school uniforms that were—literally—America's colors: red, white, and blue. Instead of raising our hands with a question for the teacher/monitor, we placed tiny American flags into slots between the desks. Our salutes to the American flag were always followed by pledges of allegiance to the Christian flag and the Holy Bible.

Overtly and subliminally, throughout my education and across the narrow spectrum of my young life, the linking of the United States and the Christian god was constant. I was part of a culture groomed to propagandize, the American flag in one hand and a Bible in the other.

Interestingly I never did hurl myself into the mission field. I never even left town. Rather I found opportunities for religious and political reinforcement in Christian echo chambers close to home, and with few exceptions, I surrounded myself with affirmation. I associated with no known atheists, and the few Democrats I brushed against seemed like foreigners who'd stumbled into the United States by accident. (The Oklahoma liberal is an anomaly rarely encountered in the wild, possibly because it's so often spooked by the sounds of native Republicans molesting their rifle triggers and beer cans.)

In my narrow perceptions, liberals were Them. The Opposition. The Other. Conservatives went to Sunday church. Liberals selfishly slept until noon. Conservatives promoted traditional family values. Liberals comingled in an orgy of sin, passing their partners around like a bong. Conservatives respected America. Liberals dismissed borders and happily gifted precious American jobs to "illegals." In all seriousness, this insipid caricature was how I once perceived the non-conservative and non-Christian, and galvanizing my worldview—day and night— was that hub of righteousness and truth-finding: Fox News. Fox was a mentor. A friend. A conduit and outlet. It simultaneously fed my perceptions and amplified them. And it constantly reminded me that I was both empowered and a victim.

Here, on the wider side of the looking glass, I'm fascinated by Fox News and the culture that feeds on it. This book is an attempt to understand and expose the faux within the Fox. It's also a retrospective, a reverse engineering of my former beliefs about the United States, its Founding Fathers, patriotism, political parties, religions, foreigners, war, protest, gays, guns, and God. You're invited to join the older/ wiser Seth Andrews as he investigates his former self and asks, "What were you thinking?"

This is my diary. This is my penance. These are the *Confessions of a Former Fox News Christian*.

CHAPTER ONE:

The Fox Phenomenon: Roger Ailes, the GOP Playbook, and the Rise of Fox News

BEFORE I DISSECT my former die-hard conservative self, it's important to lay a foundation. If we're going to understand the impact of Fox News on American culture and my evangelical past, we need to understand its players, its mission, and its origins. Those roots reach far beyond the network's 1996 launch into a turbulent, suspicious, and divided chapter of America's past. We must travel back in time. To the LBJ years. To the turbulent sixties. To the Cold War.

At the time American conservatism was withered on the vine, dormant and largely ineffectual. The economic recession of the late 1950s had fueled landslide Democratic victories in the House and Senate. The Civil Rights Movement was getting traction. Liberal notions dominated the American political landscape. Democrat John F. Kennedy had become president in 1960 before being assassinated three years later, that tragedy paving the way for Lyndon B. Johnson, who then won the 1964 presidential election by a landslide. Johnson would soon implement his Great Society, liberal programs designed to improve education, healthcare, infrastructure, housing, and poverty. Johnson's sweeping agenda had been made possible because of the popularity—and partially the martyrdom—of JFK.

John Kennedy's presidency had been made possible by a new medium—television—that had finally become commonplace in the American home. On September 26, 1960, America saw its very first televised presidential debate: Kennedy versus Republican rival Richard Nixon. The broadcast was seen by 70 million Americans, almost 40 percent of the entire population. It was a historic moment that changed U.S. politics forever.

Both men spoke with authority about the usual topics. Both were ex-military. Both served in Congress. Both expressed their political philosophies with conviction. But while radio audiences listened only to the voices of the two men, statistically calling the debate a draw, television audiences gravitated to Kennedy by a huge margin.

The reason? Nixon was terrible on television. A disaster. Next to John Kennedy—handsome, polished, born for the cameras—Richard Nixon was a sweating, shifting, blinking mess, made worse by the fact that he was exhausted and suffered flu symptoms. Nixon had committed what would become the unpardonable sin in American politics. He had looked bad on television. His failure to impress the vast viewing public resulted in his November defeat, which dealt yet another stunning blow to the Republican Party. American conservatism simply couldn't get any traction.

Nixon would run for president again in 1968. For this second campaign, he realized the need to polish his act. He needed a handler. He needed a television advisor who could get him camera-ready. Enter Nixon's media consultant Roger Ailes, future chairman and CEO of Fox News.

Roger Ailes was savvy. He understood TV as entertainment. Having majored in radio and television at Ohio University, honing his skills as an executive producer of the talk-variety program *The Mike Douglas Show*, Ailes realized that influence lay not in the presentation of facts but in playing to audience emotion. If Richard Nixon was ever going to win the White House and restore Republican power, it was critical to package the politician and the platform to target emotion. Likeability and memorability were paramount. Nixon needed to be strong and smooth. Concise and memorable. Warm and friendly. He needed to win America's heart.

Ailes went to work. He narrowed Nixon's talking points and partitioned his public speeches into sound bites. He staged tightly choreographed town hall meetings, populated the audience with Republicans, and planted "softball" questioners in the audiences.[5] (The press was barred from debate halls and forced to watch the events on a backstage monitor.) Ailes cranked the studio air conditioning at full blast to prevent Nixon from sweating.[6] He developed some of the first negative TV campaign ads, using ominous narration and stark imagery to contrast traitorous Democrats against a righteous Republican. With these strategies Roger Ailes propelled a newer, sleeker Nixon to the presidency in 1968. The failure of 1960 was forgotten. Richard Nixon had been reformatted for the television viewing public.

The following year, Roger Ailes signed his name to a "Plan for Putting the GOP on TV News," which served as a kind of Republican media bible. The manifesto declared that "people are lazy." With television, "the thinking is done for you."

A PLAN FOR PUTTING THE GOP ON TV NEWS

For 200 years the newspaper front page dominated public thinking. In the last 20 years that picture has changed. Today television news is watched more often

> than people read newspapers.
> than people listen to radio.
> than people read or gather any other form of communication.

The reason: People are lazy. With television you just sit--watch--listen. The thinking is done for you. 29% rely only on TV.

Image: DocumentCloud.org

---

5   The Nixon Effect: How Richard Nixon's Presidency Fundamentally Changed American Politics by Douglas Schoen 2016
6   Nixonland: The Rise of a President and the Fracturing of America by Rick Perlstein 2009

To embed Republican ideas into the public consciousness, Ailes implemented a specific plan "to provide pro-administration, videotape, hard news actualities to the major cities of the United States."[7] He examined the markets, guided production, and strategically offered video news packaged by "GOP people." This prefabbing of news items "avoids the censorship, the priorities, and the prejudices of network news selectors and disseminators." The Republican White House didn't want troublesome reporters going off-message, so instead, conservatives would serve canned goods to the masses. They would control the narrative by bundling their talking points in advance.

With this plan, Roger Ailes had signed a blueprint for a Republican media machine masquerading as news.

The first Nixon term was a critical time in American history. The Vietnam War raged. Civil rights protests pitched demonstrators against white supremacists. Women were petitioning for equality and opportunity beyond their stereotypical roles as homemakers and secretaries. In the turbulent 1960s and early 1970s, white male corporate dominance was being significantly challenged by a younger, more diverse counterculture generation less interested in money and industry. This change in cultural attitudes posed a threat to those in power.

In 1971 future Supreme Court justice Lewis Powell penned a memo submitted to the U.S. Chamber of Commerce claiming that the

---

CONFIDENTIAL MEMORANDUM

ATTACK ON AMERICAN FREE ENTERPRISE SYSTEM

TO: Mr. Eugene B. Sydnor, Jr.   DATE: August 23, 1971
Chairman
Education Committee
U.S. Chamber of Commerce

FROM: Lewis F. Powell, Jr.

Image: Washington and Lee University School of Law

7   "A Plan for Putting the GOP on the News" Roger Ailes 1970, Richard Nixon Presidential Library

"American economic system was under broad attack" and that political "power must be assiduously cultivated."[8]

Powell's strategy was specific: Republicans needed to install conservative professors in universities, inject conservative influence into school textbooks, activate the power of "big business," reestablish public trust in the system, counter anti-capitalist (liberal/"Marxist") doctrine, and supervise television broadcasts. Page twenty-one of the document recommended that "the national television networks should be monitored in the same way that textbooks should be kept under constant surveillance."

> **Possible Role of the Chamber of Commerce**
>
> But independent and uncoordinated activity by individual corporations, as important as this is, will not be sufficient. Strength lies in organization, in careful long-range planning and implementation, in consistency of action over an indefinite period of years, in the scale of financing available only through joint effort, and in the political power available only through united action and national organizations.

Image: Washington and Lee University School of Law

Powell's memorandum cleverly used the language of patriotism. According to his narrative, the un-American liberal elite were a threat to democracy, and drastic measures were needed to stem the lefty tide. Between those patriotic lines lay the fears over lost (white male) power and "traditional" conservative control of the culture. *Why don't non-Christians keep their mouths shut? Why can't women accept their place in the kitchen? Why won't black people sit at the back of the bus? Why won't students stop questioning our war policies? Why can't gays stay in their bathhouses? What's this country coming to?*

---

8   "Confidential Memorandum: Attack on American Free Enterprise" Lewis Powell, Jr. August 23, 1971

To consolidate power, conservative forces began selling distrust to the American people. Distrust of government. Distrust of science. Distrust of liberals. Distrust of non-sanctioned media. The Republican merchants of doubt herded the public into a journey backward, to the "good old days," to Make America Great Again. They painted America's glorious past in bright primary colors, and they blamed non-traditionalist liberals for pissing all over it.

Conservative influencers sold this story to the best of their ability, but in the 1960s and 1970s, Republican talking points were still constrained by "equal time." Under a law called the Fairness Doctrine, radio and television stations were required to balance the various points of view on their programs. This law prevented stations and their pundits from providing one-sided propaganda. If a broadcast promoted a specific opinion, that host station was forced by law to give equal time to contradicting views. As such, newscasts were largely genteel, relatively opinion-free presentations of facts from credentialed anchors such as Walter Cronkite and David Brinkley.

Then, on August 5, 1987, the Reagan administration famously struck down the Fairness Doctrine.

With the Fairness Doctrine revoked, media outlets were freed from any equal-time restrictions. Radio, television, and print media could sell a single side of any story. A year later the United States saw its first nationally syndicated right-wing talk radio program: *The Rush Limbaugh Show*. Limbaugh would set a precedent for hundreds of broadcasters to come.

Then came the Telecommunications Reform Act. That law deregulated radio and television for the supposed purpose of widening the marketplace, yet the true effect wasn't one of greater competition. Instead major media conglomerates instantly swooped in, bought up every television and radio network in sight, and established a stranglehold on American broadcasting. By 2012, 90 percent of American media was owned by just *six* companies: GE, NewsCorp,

Disney, Viacom, Time Warner, and CBS.[9]

I was a radio announcer in the 1990s, and I remember watching those major corporations vacuum up almost every frequency on the dial. My Tulsa station—KXOJ—was one of the few remaining family-owned properties in the city. Overall radio quickly became more homogenized, with the KISS-FM in one city sounding exactly like the KISS-FM in the next. Formats were rubber-stamped. Playlists were duplicated. Syndication piped in major network shows, and even the remaining local talk broadcasts were modeled on Rush Limbaugh's winning formula: opening monologue followed by callers, lots of commercial breaks, and plenty of white male outrage.

The Telecommunications Reform Act was passed in 1996. In that same year, a certain television network was launched: Fox News.

The founder of Fox News was a billionaire media mogul named Rupert Murdoch. Murdoch—an Australian—had inherited a small regional newspaper from his father and soon acquired several others across the country. In 1964 he launched Australia's only national newspaper, *The Australian*. By 1968, Murdoch had expanded his umbrella company News Corp. into the British marketplace, buying *News of the World*, the biggest newspaper in the United Kingdom. More acquisitions followed, and Murdoch expanded his media empire into the United States in 1973. He purchased the *San Antonio Express-News*, then the *New York Post*, then *Times Newspapers*. In 1985, Rupert Murdoch acquired Twentieth Century Fox, along with a large cluster of television stations that would soon comprise the Fox Television Network. (As a foreigner he was forbidden by law to own U.S. television stations, so Murdoch renounced his Australian citizenship and became a naturalized citizen of the United States.) Early Fox shows included *The Late Show* with comedian Joan Rivers, *Married with Children*, *21 Jump Street*, *The Simpsons*, *America's Most Wanted*, *Cops*, and *The X-Files*, and those shows were hugely successful.

---

9   Business Insider "These 6 Corporations Control 90 percent of the Media in America" June 14, 2012

In 1996, ten years after Rupert Murdoch launched the Fox Broadcasting Company, he founded Fox News. Fox News's first president? Roger Ailes, the man who had dreamed of "Putting the GOP on TV news."

Post Nixon, Ailes had made his own earlier attempt at a conservative news network, Television News, Inc., which failed after two years. He was a debate coach for Ronald Reagan, was actively involved in the 1988 presidential campaign of George H. W. Bush, and he advised Bush's son thirteen years later in the wake of 9/11. Ailes secretly consulted for Big Tobacco against healthcare reform soon after, and he joined CNBC as president from 1993 to 1995.

In 1996 Rupert Murdoch put Roger Ailes in the Fox News wheelhouse, and Aisles immediately went to work. He culled established media names such as Neil Cavuto, Bill O'Reilly, and Brit Hume, and he branded the channel's image in American red, white, and blue. The anchors even wore tiny American flag pins. Fox News Alerts landed like a hammer. The graphics were punchy and fast. The sound effects were bombastic. The hosts were explosive and charismatic. To engage a heavily male demographic, female sex appeal was a priority; a former Fox News contributor recalled Roger Ailes's instruction: "Tits up, hair back."[10] Ironically Ailes's Fox tenure ended under an avalanche of sexual harassment allegations; still, the new conservative flagship finally gave Roger Ailes a proper opportunity to implement the "GOP/TV News" handbook, a cultural counterpunch to the traitorous liberal onslaught, returning America to the "good old days" of "traditional American values."

Fox News promised its viewers that it would be "Fair & Balanced," which was marketing genius, because viewers would infer that all the other networks were *unfair* and *unbalanced*. Despite its equity pledge, though, a Christian nationalist narrative often spilled from the indignant mouths of mostly conservative hosts. Three of the network's biggest initial influencers—Bill O'Reilly, Sean Hannity, and

---

10   Forbes "Fox News Vets on How Roger Ailes Used Sex Appeal to Boost Ratings and Created a 'Toxic Culture' for Women" Madeline Berg, July 27, 2016

Roger Ailes's right-hand senior producer, William Shine—were Irish-Catholic firebrands, and even though Sean Hannity worked alongside liberal counterpart Alan Colmes, Colmes's mild demeanor rendered him somewhat opaque next to Hannity's boldness and bluster. (Note: Shine would go on to become Donald Trump's deputy White House chief of staff in 2018. In that same year, Hannity and Fox News's Judge Jeanine Pirro would join a Trump campaign rally in Missouri, prompting rebukes from the journalistic community. These hardline conservative political allegiances had been on proud display since the early years of Fox News.)

The network employed some progressives, but (as with Alan Colmes) liberals were often outnumbered and outshouted, producing conflict that spiked ratings and galvanized viewer perception of conservative superiority. This remains true today. For every Tamara Holder, James Carville, Kirsten Powers, or Sally Kohn (all no longer with the network), there are many more like Sean Hannity, Tomi Lahren, Newt Gingrich, Todd Starnes, Ainsley Earhardt, Tucker Carlson, Lou Dobbs, Laura Ingraham, and Mark Levin.

On October 11, 2019, the refreshingly fair Shepard Smith announced his departure from Fox News after twenty-three years. Smith was often a critic of his own network. He confirmed publicly in 2017 that he was gay (bucking other host op-eds about the "traditional family"). He defended the free press, and he was fiercely critical of untrue claims made by Donald Trump. In his prepared final statement, Shepard Smith said, "Recently I asked the company to allow me to leave Fox News and begin a new chapter. After requesting that I stay, they graciously obliged." Smith was replaced by the milder, more accommodating Bill Hemmer, who has proven much less critical of Republican talking points.

Fox News is all about warnings of attack on American values, on cherished institutions, on democracy, on the family, and on public safety. This persecution narrative strikes the nerves of American conservatives and draws them into Fox's embrace. As Alexis Fitts wrote in the *Columbia Journalism Review*, "Fox has gained this market share by its masterful manipulation of ideology, drawing an audience that's primarily conservative, and then seeking to reinforce their values."[11] Rick Perlstein, author of *Nixonland*, told *The New York Times*: "Like Richard Nixon, like Spiro Agnew, Fox News can never see itself as the attacker. They are always playing defense because they believe they are always under attack, which attracts people that have the same personality formation. By bringing that mindset, plus the high energy seamless stream of the aggression of talk radio, he [Roger Ailes] has found an audience."[12]

Crisis narratives are often used to circle the conservative wagons. Which network stoked fears about a (bogus and debunked[13]) "Ground Zero Mosque" being built at the site of the 9/11 terrorist attacks? Fox News. Which network featured horror stories about Obamacare "death panels"[14] that would deny healthcare to critically ill Americans? Fox News. Which network suggested that Hillary Clinton was an accomplice in the deadly 2012 Benghazi attacks (even as she was cleared by the Defense Department and the CIA[15])? Fox News. Which network broadcast scary stories about illegal immigrants swarming the U.S. southern border? Fox News. Which network predictably stacks its December programming with headlines about the mythical war on Christmas? Fox News. (Google the video of Megyn Kelley's 2013 rant about Santa and Jesus both being white.[16] It's awesome.)

For sheer comedy, it's hard to beat Tucker Carlson's broadcast on June 5, 2019. The object of his chagrin? The metric system. "Almost every nation on earth has fallen under the yoke of tyranny—the metric system. From Beijing to Buenos Aires, From Lusaka to London, the people of the world have been forced to measure their environment

11   Columbia Journalism Review ""And from the Left...Fox News" Alexis Sobel, March/April 2014
12   New York Times "A Fox Chief at the Pinnacle of Media and Politics" by David Carr and Tim Arango, January 9, 2010
13   Snopes "Is the 'Ground Zero Mosque' Project Back?" December 19, 2019
14   Fox News "Hannity" July 20, 2013
15   U.S. House of Representatives "The Select Committee on Benghazi" December 7, 2016
16   Fox News The Kelly File December 11, 2013

in millimeters and kilograms." Carlson's guest for the segment, James Panero, called the metric system "the original system of global revolution and new world orders."

At Fox News, even *math* is an attack on America.

Returning to President Obama, in 2012 *Fox & Friends* broadcasted a four-minute video produced in-house called "Four Years of Hope and Change," which painted Barack Obama against stark imagery, danger music, and troubling warnings about the national debt, impending economic collapse, and more. This hit piece was presented as news, but it came off like a Republican campaign commercial. The clip was so problematic that Fox News immediately removed the video from every place it had been posted, replaced it with an edited video, and then yanked the edited version. (Fortunately the Internet never forgets. The clip is still out there.)

Fox has gotten considerable mileage out of Obama the Democrat Darling, and it has been so deferential to Donald Trump that the rare unflattering story has prompted Trump's Twitter outrage. A 2019 Fox News poll showed 50 percent of Americans choosing Joe Biden over Donald Trump for the 2020 election. Fifty-six percent disapproved of Trump's performance, and 59 percent declared that he was "tearing the country apart."[17] Trump's response was hugely revealing.

 **Donald J. Trump** ✓
@realDonaldTrump

....I don't want to Win for myself, I only want to Win for the people. The New @FoxNews is letting millions of GREAT people down! We have to start looking for a new News Outlet. Fox isn't working for us anymore!

9:03 AM · Aug 28, 2019 · Twitter for iPhone

---

17   Fox News poll August 11 – 13

Fox isn't working for him anymore?

To his credit, the following day Fox News host Neil Cavuto respond-ed, "President Trump, Fox News doesn't work for you." On Twitter, Brit Hume said the same:

Brit Hume ✓
@brithume

Fox News isn't supposed to work for you.

9:06 AM · Aug 28, 2019 · Twitter for iPad

But Trump's attitude toward the network said everything. Until August 2019, he had remained relatively coddled by Fox News. Trump had given far more interviews on Fox than any other network and was an avid viewer. When he was strangely, finally, presented with an uncomplimentary story, Trump felt thrown under the bus. Years of rev-erential Fox News "reporting" had conditioned him to expect being shown only in the best light. Fox was a Trump ally. Fox was a con-servative bastion. Fox was an extension of the GOP. In 2007 famed broadcaster Larry King would say as much to the *Chicago Sun-Times*, declaring that Fox News is "a Republican brand. They're an exten-sion of the Republican Party with some exceptions [like] Greta Van Susteren."[18] A decade later Rupert Murdoch's own son James would lament that Fox News often devolved into a conservative soapbox with little interest in truth.[19] In 2019, political correspondent Julia Ioffe called Fox News "Dear Leader state-run TV."

The 2020 COVID-19 pandemic provided an interesting example of the message parallel between Fox News and the Trump White House. Before Donald Trump declared a national emergency on March 13, he had spent two months dismissing the crisis, boasting

---

18   Chicago Sun-Times interview January 17, 2007
19   New York Times "How Rupert Murdoch's Empire Remade the World" April 3, 2019

---

that the United States had "pretty much shut it down coming from China"[20] and that Democrats were merely politicizing COVID-19 as "their new hoax."[21]

The Fox News machine largely echoed that narrative. After a sarcastic February monologue about how "the sky is absolutely falling" and "you're going to die, all of you in the next forty-eight hours," Sean Hannity blasted Democrats and the media for "scaring people unnecessarily."[22] He displayed a chart showing zero COVID-19 deaths in the United States. Jeanine Pirro dismissed notions that COVID-19 might be more dangerous than the flu.[23] *Fox & Friends'* Ainsley Earhardt gleefully encouraged viewers to travel: "It's actually the safest time to fly."[24] Pete Hegseth of *Fox & Friends Weekend* said, "I feel like the more I learn about this, the less there is to worry about."[25] Lou Dobbs accused the "national left-wing media" of using COVID-19 to crash the stock market.[26] Laura Ingraham's on-screen chyron read "Trump Confronts the Panic Pushers" as she assured her audience that "the risks to the average person does remain quite low."[27] Tomi Lahren sneered, "But now the sky is falling because we have a few dozen cases of coronavirus on a cruise ship?"[28] *Fox Business*'s Trish Regan accused the liberal media of using "coronavirus in an attempt to demonize and destroy the president." (Regan's on-screen chyron read "Coronavirus Impeachment Scam.")[29]

On March 16, three days after the White House declared a national emergency, President Trump shifted to starker references to "an invisible enemy"[30] and, on the following day, boasted that "I felt it was a pandemic long before it was called a pandemic."[31] At his April

20 Fox News interview on "Hannity" Feb 3, 2020
21 Trump South Carolina campaign rally Feb 28, 2020
22 Fox News "Hannity" Feb 27, 2020
23 Justice with Judge Jeanine March 7, 2020
24 Fox & Friends March 13, 2020
25 Fox & Friends Saturday March 8, 2020
26 Fox Business "Lou Dobbs Tonight" March 9, 2020
27 Fox News, March 10, 2020
28 Fox Nation "Final Thoughts," March 10, 2020
29 Fox Business, March 9, 2020
30 Trump news conference, March 16, 2020
31 Trump news conference, March 17, 2020

4 news conference Trump warned, "There will be a lot of death, unfortunately."[32]

As if lashed to Trump by a tether, Fox News suddenly joined the chorus of dire warnings about the seriousness of the COVID-19 situation. Doing damage control, Sean Hannity rewrote his own history by declaring, "This program has always taken the coronavirus seriously."[33] Jeanine Pirro referenced "an incredibly contagious and dangerous virus."[34] Ainsley Earhardt switched gears only four days after her great-time-to-fly statements with the somber prompt, "We have a responsibility to slow down this virus and to think of other people during this time."[35] Lou Dobbs self-quarantined on March 21 after a staffer tested positive for COVID-19. And only eight days after her "impeachment scam" rant, Trish Regan declared, "It's critical we know who has this. We must test for the virus in order to stop the spread of it."[36] (On March 27, *Fox Business* dropped Regan's program after fierce public criticism of her original comments.)

Certainly, there were exceptions to the Trump-Fox link. Tucker Carlson (of all people!) sounded the alarm bells early, even attempting to influence President Trump to take the crisis more seriously. But largely, Donald Trump and Fox News spent the first quarter of 2020 as dance partners, dismissing concerns, harrumphing about conspiracy, and blaming liberals and reporters for blowing things out of proportion. On April 5, 2020, nearly eighty journalism professors from across the nation published an "Open Letter to the Murdochs," declaring Fox News's misinformation "a danger to public health."[37] The next day, *Vanity Fair* reported that Fox News was preparing for "a litany of public-interest lawsuits and letters of condemnation for pedaling misinformation for weeks prior to coronavirus's explosion in the U.S."[38]

---

32 Trump news conference, April 4, 2020
33 Sean Hannity, "Hannity," March 18, 2020
34 "Justice with Jeanine Pirro," March 14, 2020
35 Fox & Friends, March 17, 2020
36 Fox Business, March 13, 2020
37 Letter posted by reporter Oliver Darcy on Twitter, April 1, 2020 @oliverdarcy
38 Vanity Fair, "Fox News Is Preparing to be Sued over Coronavirus Misinformation"

Further examples of Fox's suspiciously cozy relationship with the Republican White House? *Business Insider* recently examined the revolving door between the Trump administration and Fox News, and it's hugely revealing:[39]

- Hope Hicks served as White House communications director before being hired as Fox News's senior public relations executive. In 2020 she is returning as a White House senior advisor.

- Sarah Sanders, former White House press secretary, joined Fox News as a commentator in 2019.

- Former White House Deputy Press Secretary Raj Shah became a senior vice president at Fox in July 2019.

- Former Trump Deputy Campaign Manager David Bossie is a Fox analyst.

- Trump's former Acting ICE Director Thomas Homan became a Fox News contributor in June 2018.

- Former Fox News executive Bill Shine worked for the Trump administration as chief of staff for communications and is an advisor for Trump's 2020 election campaign.

- *Fox & Friends* host Heather Nauert was Department of State spokesperson from 2017 to 2019. She was replaced in April 2019 by Morgan Ortagus, another Fox News contributor.

- Transportation Secretary Elaine Chao has been a Fox News contributor and served on the board of Fox's parent company, News Corp.

- Short-term White House Communications Director Anthony Scaramucci previously hosted *Wall Street Week* on Fox News.

---

39 Business Insider "Hope Hicks is Returning to the White House" February 13, 2020

- Former Trump personal aide John McEntee was a former Fox production assistant.

- Treasury Department Spokesperson Tony Sayegh was a GOP strategist and Fox News contributor before joining the Trump administration.

- U.S. Ambassadors Scott Brown, Richard Grenell, and Georgette Mosbacher all worked as Fox contributors before taking their government positions.

There are other examples, revealing a frequent crossing of the streams between a Republican administration and a supposed model of journalistic objectivity.

Of course, no news network is bias free, because no person is bias free. Ad Fontes Media conducted an extensive study of media bias, with Fox News (obviously) well to the right, along with *NewsMax*, *The Washington Examiner*, *Breitbart*, *CNS News*, *The Blaze*, and *The American Spectator*. Liberal outlets included MSNBC, *Daily Kos*, *Vanity Fair*, *Washington Monthly*, and *Alternet*. CNN broadcast was closer to center but still distinctly left. Scoring high marks for fairness, depth, and accuracy were *Business Insider*, *CBS News*, *CNN Online*, *The Economist*, *Forbes*, *The Hill*, NPR, *The Wall Street Journal*, *The Washington Post*, and *The New York Times*.[40]

But we must look at the larger picture of how news is acquired by the American viewing public. Statistically the conservatives are more likely to lean on a *single news source*, where liberals are more likely to get their information from *several sources*. During the 2016 presidential election, Fox News was the main news source for a full 40 percent of Trump voters.[41] Conversely the top 40 percent of voters for Hillary Clinton used a wider array of outlets such as CNN, MSNBC, Facebook, and even local television. In these figures we can see the culling of conservative audiences into the narrow informational

---

40   Ad Fontes Media "Interactive Media Bias Chart 5.0" 2019
41   Pew Research Center "Trump, Clinton Voters Divided in their Main Source for Election News" January 18, 2017

conduit. Fox News viewers are groomed to feel superior, warned of constant danger, showered with patriotic glitter, and affirmed in their largely conservative political convictions.

Fox News viewer indignation is often rooted in ignorance and disinformation and the embrace of belief over knowledge. Many possess a Dunning-Kruger illusion of superiority rooted in cognitive bias, defiantly declaring the supremacy of their opinion over another's facts. As Tim Dickenson said in *Rolling Stone*:

> *The result of this concerted campaign of disinformation is a viewership that knows almost nothing about what's going on in the world. According to recent polls, Fox News viewers are the most misinformed of all news consumers. They are 12 percentage points more likely to believe the stimulus package caused job losses, 17 points more likely to believe Muslims want to establish Shariah law in America, 30 points more likely to say that scientists dispute global warming, and 31 points more likely to doubt President Obama's citizenship. In fact, a study by the University of Maryland reveals, ignorance of Fox viewers actually increases the longer they watch the network. That's because [Roger] Ailes isn't interested in providing people with information, or even a balanced range of perspectives. Like his political mentor, Richard Nixon, Ailes traffics in the emotions of victimization.*[42]

Fox News's ratings success has become the icing on the cake. Fox crushed all the other news outlets as the top cable news network in the last quarter of 2019. It was its seventy-first ratings quarter at number one, with an average of 2.4 million primetime viewers from eight to eleven o'clock at night.[43] (Note the hosts for this three-hour block: Tucker Carlson, Sean Hannity, and Laura Ingraham, all conservative firebrands doing editorial content.) This overwhelming success has a reinforcing effect for the Fox audience. *"If Fox News is so bad, why is*

---

42 Rolling Stone "How Roger Ailes Built the Fox News Fear Factory" June 9, 2011
43 Neilson Media Research December 2019

it so successful?" This phenomenon is known as the "appeal to popularity," the idea that a claim is accepted as being true simply because most people are favorably inclined toward it. Most people approve of X; therefore, X must be true.

Other chapters in this book delve deeper into how right-wing talk radio, Bible teaching, and even brain physiology can help to reinforce this kind of political tunnel vision, but we've laid the foundation for how Fox News both feeds on and feeds into American conservatism and Christian nationalism. There is news, and there is Fox News, and the two are often not the same thing.

If I can digress for a moment, there is also compelling evidence that the network is not a safe place for females. Former Fox News host Gretchen Carlson filed a 2016 sexual harassment lawsuit against Roger Ailes (who incidentally died of hemophilia the following year). Her suit claimed that Ailes had harassed her and several other women and that she was fired after refusing his advances. Carlson won a $20 million settlement and an apology from Fox News for not treating her "with the respect that she and all our colleagues deserve."[44] Carlson's suit allegedly prompted an internal investigation at Fox, but it appears that Fox used Carlson's nondisclosure agreement to silence her, pushing her into private arbitration instead of the public court system.

After Carlson's suit there was an avalanche of sexual harassment allegations against Roger Ailes and Fox News, with more than twenty women reportedly speaking to lawyers about Ailes's inappropriate behavior. Host Megyn Kelly has been public about Roger Ailes's advances toward her. Guest booker Laurie Luhn told *New York Magazine* that Ailes "psychologically tortured her" for twenty years as she acquiesced to receiving career opportunities in exchange for sexual favors. Other Ailes targets included host Andrea Tantaros, reporter Rudi Bakhtiar, producer Shelley Ross, advisor Kellie Boyle, and many others who would speak only anonymously to authorities. (The

---

44   NPR "Former Fox Host Gretchen Carlson Gets Apology, $20M Settlement" September 6, 2016

2019 film *Bombshell* is a dramatization of the Carlson lawsuit against the backdrop of Ailes's predation on the females of Fox News.)

Another set of incidents involved prime time host Bill O'Reilly, who—with Fox News—settled six sexual harassment lawsuits to the tune of $50 million and was dropped by the network. Both Ailes and O'Reilly protested their innocence, but the testimony against them was overwhelming and the settlements very telling. The "traditional family values" network was apparently a haven for sexual predation.

Roger Ailes may be gone, but the Fox News juggernaut remains, with no sign that it plans to change its long-winning formula. It will likely continue to sail its ship on a conservative tide. It will continue to dazzle its viewers with flash and bombast. It will stoke the fires of controversy and indignation. It will remain a dance partner with a Republican White House. And it will wrestle to sell its family-friendly veneer against the payouts and settlements on behalf of alleged sexual predators.

CHAPTER TWO:

The Rush to Anger: Conservative Talk Radio and the Angry White Male

IN THE EARLY weeks of the NFL pro football season, it was the Philadelphia Eagles versus the Buffalo Bills. It was September 28, 2003.

The ESPN sports network had been in hot water for its recent hiring of controversial conservative talk radio giant Rush Limbaugh as a pundit, and as the TV cameras rolled on ESPN's *Sunday NFL Countdown*, the water boiled over.

The conversation had turned to Eagles quarterback Donovan McNabb. The panel (also consisting of Steve Young, Michael Irvin, Tom Jackson, and Chris Berman) wondered if McNabb's performance as an athlete had been regressing. Sure, his team had won the game, but had Donovan McNabb been the cornerstone for the win? Did the quarterback genuinely deserve so much credit? Rush Limbaugh, unfortunately, offered his opinion. He made the discussion about race:

> I'm sorry to say this, I don't think he's been that good from the get-go. What we have here is a little social concern in the NFL. The media has been very desirous that a black quarterback can do well, black coaches and black quarterbacks

doing well. There is a little hope invested in McNabb, and he got a lot of credit for the performance of this team that he didn't deserve. The defense carried this team.[45]

Rush's cohosts deftly skirted the racial portion of his claim and returned the conversation to athleticism and playmaking, but the damage had been done. Limbaugh was asserting that Donovan McNabb was an overrated player protected by the NFL establishment because he was black, and the NFL was merely trying to sell a public image of diversity at the QB position. (In fact, 2003 saw black quarterbacks starting at least one game in ten of its thirty-two teams.[46])

Rush's little editorial cost him the job. After political pressure from a few dozen U.S. House politicians and an avalanche of public outrage, ESPN accepted Limbaugh's resignation. The remaining *Sunday NFL Countdown* hosts faced public criticism for letting Rush's rant go unchallenged, and on the following broadcast, Tom Jackson admitted as much:

> Rush Limbaugh is known for the divisive nature of his rhetoric. He creates controversy, and what he said Sunday is the same type of thing that he said on radio for years. A player in this league who has a young son called me this week, and his son now wants to know if it's all right for blacks to play quarterback. Rush Limbaugh's comments could not have been more hurtful. He was brought in to talk football, and he broke that trust.[47]

Interestingly *The New York Times* reported that Limbaugh's final *Sunday NFL Countdown* was the highest-rated episode in seven years.[48]

---

45   ESPN Sunday Countdown broadcast September 28, 2003
46   ESPN "Limbaugh's Comments Touch Off Controversy" October 1, 2003
47   ESPN Sunday Countdown broadcast October 5, 2003
48   The New York Times "FOOTBALL; Limbaugh Resigns from ESPN's NFL Show" October 2, 2003

So what happened that day? Did Rush simply, accidentally, misspeak? Of course not. Limbaugh told millions exactly what he was thinking.

Earlier that same year, hardcore conservative Michael Savage paid a similar price. Savage had built his significant *Savage Nation* radio audience under original slogan, "To the right of Rush and to the left of God," and he frequently gave his Bronx cheer to undocumented immigrants ("brown supremacists"), gays ("the homosexual mafia"), and the Left ("socialists"). Savage ranted about "turd world nations" and warned that the United States was "being taken over by the freaks, the cripples, the perverts, and the mental defectives."[49] (Note the title of his 2005 book, *Liberalism Is a Mental Disorder*, and notice the publisher, Thomas Nelson, the leading world provider of Bibles and Christian books.)

Over the objections of employees, MSNBC President Erik Sorenson hired Michael Savage for a one-hour television talk show. Sorenson thought Savage's style would translate well to television, and he likely felt the pot-stirring firebrand would bring a ratings punch to his meandering news network. He was immediately warned of calamity by organizations such as the Gay and Lesbian Alliance Against Defamation, which had already led an advertiser boycott of Savage's radio talk show.

The concerns were warranted. It took Michael Savage only four months to torpedo his MSNBC gig. On the July 7, 2003, broadcast, a prank caller insulted Savage's teeth. Bristling from behind his sunglasses, the host responded:

> Oh, so you're one of those sodomites. You should only get AIDS and die, you pig. How's that? Why don't you see if you can sue me, you pig? You got nothing better to do than to put me down, you piece of garbage? You got nothing to do today?

---

49   Weapons of Mass Deception: The Uses of Propaganda in Bush's War on Iraq by Sheldon Rampton 2003

Go eat a sausage and choke on it. Get trichinosis. Now do we have another nice caller here who's busy because he didn't have a nice night in the bathhouse who's angry at me today? Put another, put another sodomite on. No more calls? I don't care about these bums. They mean nothing to me. They're all sausages.[50]

Watch the YouTube video clip of the exchange, and you can taste the bile.

MSNBC quickly pulled the plug, and Michael Savage groped for an excuse. Apologizing the next day on his radio show, he argued that he thought MSNBC had gone to commercial. (I'm not sure how this excuses the behavior.) Savage also explained, "I meant to insult him [the caller] personally, not all people with AIDS."[51]

What is surprising is that anyone found this outburst surprising. Michael Savage had built his empire on Mount Antipathy, and even his termination from MSNBC didn't slow his goose step. In his 2004 book, *The Savage Nation*, Savage called MSNBC reporter Ashleigh Banfield a "mind slut with a big pair of glasses." He lamented that Latinos "breed like rabbits" and called Supreme Court Justice Ruth Bader Ginsburg "a radical left-wing, buck-toothed hag."[52]

The cases of Rush Limbaugh and Michael Savage reveal an interesting phenomenon. These radio powerhouses enjoy monumental—even historic—success within the relatively closed systems of conservative talk radio stations, yet when they attempt to play beyond their primary sandboxes, they almost immediately self-destruct or find themselves scrambling against public contempt. Fortunately for them, talk radio is a relatively confined hub for conservative male discontent Where liberal talk experiments have crashed and burned (Ed Schultz, Randi Rhodes, Alan Colmes, etc.), conservative talk shows constitute a huge piece of the radio pie. *Talkers Magazine* published its 2019

---

50   The Savage Nation MSNBC July 7, 2003
51   The Savage Nation radio show July 8, 2003
52   SF Gate "Savage Says He's Sorry—But Stays Fired" Dan Fost, July 9, 2003

Heavy Hundred list, ranking the most powerful and influential hosts in the United States. The top five are as follows:[53]

1) **Sean Hannity** (Christian conservative)

2) **Rush Limbaugh** (Christian conservative)

3) **Dave Ramsey** (Christian conservative)

4) **Mark Levin** (Christian conservative)

5) **Howard Stern** (Whew! Finally, a liberal.)

In the *Talkers* listing, Fox News's Brian Kilmeade ranked number seven. Glenn Beck rounded out the top ten. Former National Rifle Association spokesperson Dana Loesch ranked number seventeen. Michael Savage was number twenty. In terms of specific listener numbers, the rankings play out like a Greatest Hits of white conservative males: Rush Limbaugh (15 million), Sean Hannity (15 million), Dave Ramsey (13 million), Michael Savage (11 million), Glenn Beck (10.5 million), Mark Levin (10 million).

Forbes Magazine published a 2015 op-ed pondering "Why All The Talk-Radio Stars Are Conservative." The article explored the liberal trends toward media outlets like *The New York Times*, *The Washington Post*, and *NPR* (dubbed The Mainstream Media by skeptics). Conservative talkers have constructed a business model that lambasts The Mainstream Media as corrupt and biased, effectively stoking attitudes of suspicion and drawing listeners further into an information bubble. Ironically, like Fox News, they often do so by claiming to balance the scales. Rush Limbaugh famously says, "I don't need equal time. I *am* equal time!"[54] He's also on record calling government, academia, science, and the media "the Four Corners of Deceit."[55]

The message is simple: *You can't trust them. But you can trust me.* This is a common applause line among American conservatives.

---

53 Talkers "2019 Heavy Hundred" 2019
54 The Rush Limbaugh Show "Rush Quotes" January 17, 2007
55 Rush Limbaugh radio show November 24, 2009

Former vice presidential candidate Sarah Palin constantly rips the "lamestream media." In 2020, when a CNN reporter approached Arizona Senator Martha McSally to inquire about evidence in the Trump impeachment trial, McSally responded, "You're a liberal hack. I'm not talking to you."

Donald Trump constantly cries "fake news." At his 2018 speech before the Veterans of Foreign Wars Convention in Kansas City, Trump said, "Just remember, what you are seeing and what you are reading is not what's happening." I'm reminded of that line from George Orwell, "The Party told you to reject the evidence of your eyes and ears. It was their final, most essential command."[56]

Joel Schumacher's 1993 film *Falling Down* provides some commentary on America's Angry White Male. In the movie Michael Douglas's character, William Foster, grows increasingly unhinged in the wake of his own misfortunes and feelings of persecution. He loses his job. His ex-wife takes out a restraining order. He sneers at high retail prices and rants about a fast-food burger that looks nothing like the restaurant photos. He is accosted by a gang. He acquires weapons. He shoots up various establishments by accident or in frustration. He ultimately realizes he is the villain of his own story, gives up, and manipulates a police officer into killing him.

To be fair, Foster's motivations aren't driven by white supremacy (he's disgusted by the bigotry of an army surplus store owner), but he reflects the white male discontent felt by many American men: *The American Dream was not as advertised. It's all going wrong. Humanity is circling the drain. The time for half-measures is over.*

Cognitive neuroscientist Dr. Bobby Azarian has examined common attitudes among political groups. In a 2016 *Psychology Today* column he examines trends in the Right and the Left, and those trends are very telling.[57]

---

56   1984 George Orwell June 1949
57   Psychology Today "Fear and Anxiety Drive Conservatives' Political Attitudes" December 31, 2016

- Conservatives are more prone to focus on the negative. When shown both positive and negative photographs, liberals were drawn more toward the good (happy children, cute animals) while conservatives tended to dwell on the awful (car accidents, open wounds). This "negativity bias" produces a heightened sense of danger. Threats seem bigger. The world looks more dangerous.

- Conservatives have a stronger physiological response to threats. In short, the data suggests that they scare more easily. In an unsafe world, they embrace a worldview that provides a feeling of safety. (This explains much of the gun culture in America.)

- Conservatives are more prone to fearing new experiences. While liberals own more books, travel more, and often seek adventure, conservatives are more inclined toward habit, seclusion, and orderliness.

- Conservatives appear physically wired to be more reactive to fear. An MRI study at the University College London discovered a larger amygdala in people who identified as conservative. The amygdala is the part of the brain that processes emotion, and it's "especially reactive to fearful stimuli."

This last trend has been borne out in an earlier brain study conducted at Emory University. Psychologist Drew Westen determined that while Republicans and Democrats were both prone to in-group bias, Republicans supporting a political candidate were (marginally) more likely to insulate their own candidate while calling out hypocrisy in the opposition. As answers to various questions were given, MRI scans revealed that partisans were leaning on the "emotional" rather than "logical" parts of the brain. Westen chronicled these results in his 2008 book, *The Political Brain: The Role of Emotion in Deciding the Fate of the Nation*.

This kind of protectionism extends to ideas. A 2008 Pew Research

Center study revealed that Republicans were 23 percent less likely to change their minds when being educated about climate science.[58] Even intelligent, college-degreed Republicans were statistically more likely to rationalize their positions. To quote science author Chris Mooney, they become "smart idiots," more biased and less persuadable. Conservatives are more likely to double down on an initial conviction, maneuvering their arguments in clever ways to fit the square peg into the round hole. The brain's emotion centers have blended the opinion into their identity, so an attack on the idea is a threat to the person. (All human beings are prone to this way of thinking, but again, we're seeing more of it among Republicans.)

If conservative brains respond more quickly (and more strongly) to emotional appeals, it becomes easier to understand the evocative power of political ads, especially those playing to notions of American pride, security, dominance, and destiny. *Candidate X will stand up against Big Government. Candidate X will protect your Second Amendment Right. Candidate X will promote Christian values. Candidate X is tough on crime. Candidate X will strengthen borders. Candidate X will stand against "un-American" values.*

Many of us have a healthy cynicism about political advertisements. Most of them appear to have been mass produced in an election factory. (I spent twenty years in radio and video production. I've made several of these commercials.) Positive ads are airbrushed in patriotic colors as the candidate eats cornbread with small-town citizens. Negative ads are grainy black-and-white horror films about the corruption and treason of The Other Guy. Most of these ads are—necessarily, I admit—skimpy on details about a candidate's specific platforms and plans. Instead, these commercials are broad caresses of America's heartstrings. They're targeting viewer emotion, and fear is a hugely powerful emotion. Fear of change. Fear of harm. Fear of the Other. Even fear of conflicting information that might produce palpable mental discomfort (cognitive dissonance).

---

58 Pew Research Center "A Deeper Partisan Divide Over Global Warming" May 8, 2008

Fortunately for the Fox News Christian, conservative talk radio provides plenty of affirmation. Rush Limbaugh's audience agrees with him so frequently that they call themselves "dittoheads." America is a Christian nation? *Ditto.* Guns are a human/American right? *Ditto.* Immigrants are threatening American jobs? *Ditto.* Climate science is bogus? *Ditto.* Liberals want to dismantle our republic? *Ditto.*

I was once a dittohead. My own radio career began in 1990. I worked for a Tulsa Christian music station, mostly spinning disks, giving the time and weather, and talking about benign lifestyle topics. When my air shift was finished, I caught Rush Limbaugh's broadcast on AM740 KRMG during the drive home. I didn't care for the caller segments, but Rush would populate the first fifteen minutes of every hour with a can't-miss monologue that pressed all my Republican buttons. I'd begin the commute in relative relaxation. By the time I arrived home, I'd be coiled up like a spring. My amygdala was effectively engaged.

Limbaugh began his national broadcast on August 1, 1988, graduating to the big leagues after experiencing massive local success in Sacramento, California. Rush's national launch was wedged between the 1988 presidential conventions, and his meteoric rise aligned with the 1990 Gulf War. He was lightning in a bottle. By the time the Limbaugh empire had expanded to 650 stations nationwide, he had become the darling of the Republican party. Rush's philosophies had been succinctly summed up in his 1988 article penned for *The Sacramento Union* titled "Undeniable Truths" (still posted proudly on the **rushlimbaugh.com** website). Just a few of the points follow.

- Ours is a world governed by the aggressive use of force.

- There is only one way to get rid of nuclear weapons: use them.

- Freedom is God given.

- The Peace Movement in the United States—whether by accident or design—is pro-communist.

- Evolution cannot explain creation.

- Feminism was established to allow unattractive women access to the mainstream of society.

- There will always be poor people. This is not the fault of the rich.

- You should thank God for making you an American, and instead of feeling guilty about it, help spread our ideas worldwide.

I never stopped to unpack these troubling claims. Instead, I was emboldened by Rush's fearless rhetoric about dominance. Of course I didn't want nuclear war, but I was convinced that half measures guaranteed defeat. If victory meant leaning on The Button (especially if it resulted in non-American casualties only), so be it. I swelled with pride at Limbaugh's defiant defense of the armed forces, unaware of the irony that Rush had enjoyed a deferment from any military service. Even more ironically, the first hour of Rush Limbaugh's radio show was broadcast every weekday on the Armed Forces Radio Network.

I was a devout Christian who considered divorce a sin, yet I was untroubled by Limbaugh's multiple marriages (in the 1990s, he was on his third of four wives). I claimed a desire for gender equality, but I had bought into the Limbaugh lie that "feminazis" were man-hating malcontents, and I recoiled when Gloria Steinem talked about "revolution." Rush often boasted he was a fan of the Women's Movement— when he was walking behind it. He also claimed that "women still live longer than men because their lives are easier."[59]

I had no children, but I was vehemently anti-abortion. When Rush Limbaugh's 1992 bestselling book claimed that "militant feminists are pro-choice because it's their ultimate avenue of power over men,"[60] I blindly accepted the notion that feminists sought to eliminate the rights of fathers even as they murdered their unborn. My own mother

---

59   Rush Limbaugh radio show March 1, 2005
60   The Way Things Ought to Be Rush Limbaugh 1992

predicted that conservatives would breed themselves into statistical dominance, because liberals were aborting future generations. I had never known a woman who'd had an abortion. I had never been faced with an unwanted pregnancy or impending birth defect. I laughed when Rush Limbaugh suddenly cut off unwanted callers with "caller abortions." I'm ashamed of my callousness.

Rush's lampooning of homosexuals fortified my biblically informed view that gays were in rebellion against God and destined for Hell. I commonly used "gay" as a slur: *That's so gay. Don't be gay. You're being totally gay!* (As I mention in a later chapter, this attitude would shatter after I was confronted with my own bigotry.)

In the early 1990s, my knowledge of AIDS was pathetically limited; I considered it "the gay disease." I had little sympathy for the tens of thousands infected with HIV, not because I consciously hated homosexuals, but because my empathy was dulled by "hate the sin/love the sinner" piety. As such, when Rush quipped about AIDS prevention by not asking "another man to bend over and make love at the exit point,"[61] I smirked with nonchalance. Sure, people were dying, but they weren't my people, and it wasn't my problem. The problem was that the victims weren't straight, conservative, or Christian. They needed to get their lives right. They needed Jesus.

My social circles were colorless. I was as white as my friends, and they were as white as their friends. I had enjoyed the privilege of a middle-class home, private schools, and plenty of relationship and career opportunities, and yet I somehow felt that persecution lay just over every horizon. Except for a few black conservatives like Alan Keyes and Clarence Thomas, black Americans leaned heavily into the Democratic party, linking them in my mind. The Democrats were Jesse Jackson. The Democrats were Al Sharpton. The Democrats were liberals, and liberals were un-American. Even as I was freshly emerging from my religious faith in 2008, I remained in opposition to presidential candidate Barack Obama over his liberal ideas. In 2007,

---

61   Rush to Excellence speaking tour 1989

Rush referred to Obama—whose mother was white—as a "halfrican American." Later that same year, Limbaugh's show featured a parody song titled "Barack the Magic Negro." I resisted the racial slurs, but I resisted the Democratic Party even more.

I was a Christian Dominionist. I believed that the Earth and all its resources were created by God for the pleasure and purpose of man. As the Bible said, "The highest heavens belong to the LORD, but the Earth he has given to humankind" (Psalm 115:16). The land was ours. The animals were ours. The oil was ours. The forests were ours. And it was arrogant to believe that humans could ever have a lasting negative global impact. When Limbaugh claimed that volcanic eruptions disproved all notions of human-caused climate change[62] (producing more ozone-depleting chemicals in one burst than the whole industrialized world), I nodded in approval. No need to consult actual climate scientists. Those lefty university elites were part of the Four Corners of Deceit.

Rush Limbaugh championed the idea of the Rugged Individualist, his attitude perhaps best encapsulated in a statement on his September 7, 2010, radio monologue:

> America was built by people who fended for themselves, who expected nothing from the government except protection. They expected nothing from the government except protection from foreign enemies and a just rule of law. Other than that, stay the hell out of our lives.

There's some truth to the claim that Rush became a ratings giant on talent and hard work, but he was born in the American heartland in a family of lawyers and was never forced to walk in the shoes of a suppressed minority. He hadn't been rejected from a job or pulled over in a vehicle because of his skin color. He hadn't received a smaller paycheck or been sexually harassed because he was a woman. He never feared physical harm because he was gay or transsexual.

---

62   The Way Things Ought to Be Rush Limbaugh 1992

Beyond that, Limbaugh's attitudes reflected the 1960s attitudes of Robert Welch, founder of the conservative extremist group the John Birch Society. JBS was a radical conservative group formed during the paranoia of the Cold War. It opposed the civil rights movement. It opposed the Equal Rights Amendment (part of a "communist plot"[63]). It warned of a One World Government. The John Birch Society was so extreme that even conservative icon William F. Buckley, Jr., kept his distance. Robert Welch often waxed nostalgic for the earlier, simpler days of 1900, when Rugged Individualism culled the successful from the failed, the rich from the poor, the powerful from the weak. It was the time before social programs like welfare. Women couldn't vote. Child labor laws didn't exist. Homosexuals were called sodomites. The country was racially segregated. The good old days.

Welch's philosophy was an economically Darwinian one: survival of the fittest. Sure, some people were poor, but if they didn't propel themselves into The American Dream, it was their own fault. In fact, their low status would be a healthy motivator to rise and overcome, and if anyone fell through the cracks, it was merely the price of liberty, collateral damage. This was Limbaugh's doctrine, rooted in a mythical past, and it—obviously—favored white men.

In this sense, Rush and I had much in common. On our perches of privilege, we claimed that success and/or failure was completely the responsibility of those who simply needed to buck up and pull themselves up by their bootstraps. (Like or dislike her, New York Representative Alexandria Ocasio-Cortez was absolutely correct when she tweeted that "It's a physical impossibility to lift yourself up by a bootstrap."[64] Indeed there are many who are genuinely—tragically—locked into cycles of poverty and misery. The socially disadvantaged can bootstrap until their hands are bloody, but they remain hamstrung by circumstance and the system.)

Perhaps what's most notable about the popularity of hosts like Rush

---

63   Justice and Gender by Deborah L. Rhode 1989
64   Twitter @AOC February 6, 2020

Limbaugh and Michael Savage isn't their huge ratings. Shock radio has long used controversy to get attention. What's most striking is the constant—even gleeful—absence of empathy. Rush Limbaugh's audience is 80 percent conservative (mostly men),[65] which brings us back to their statistically greater aversion to out-group acceptance. How often have Limbaugh and Savage pitched themselves and their audiences against the Other: the liberal, the gay, the feminist, the black, the Muslim, and more? Conservative talk radio has a reinforcing effect. The more you listen, the more you distrust the outside world. The more you distrust the outside world, the more you listen. It doesn't take long before your world is a terrarium.

Rush Limbaugh paved the way for Fox News, which paved the way for President Donald Trump. Limbaugh and Trump are eerily similar. They both avoided the draft while waxing about military action. They've both race-baited black Americans and linked whiteness to the national identity. They've promoted distrust of journalists. They think climate science is a scam. They've warned that "political correctness" will destroy everything America stands for. They're both petty and cruel to others. And they've cultivated an angry, paranoid, often alarmingly ignorant and bigoted audience clutching desperately to its god and guns.

Filmmaker Jen Senko produced a fascinating 2016 documentary called *The Brainwashing of My Dad*. Senko's father, Frank, was once a "nonpolitical Kennedy Democrat" until he started listening to Rush Limbaugh in the 1990s. Frank became obsessed with conservative talk radio. He devoured Rush Limbaugh on his long daytime commutes, and he huddled with his headphones for evening shows by other right-wing hosts. His wife and children watched in alarm as he acted more and more like a member of a cult.

Frank Senko became increasingly isolated and agitated, addicted to outrage. After long Limbaugh sessions in the car, Senko would rant

---

65 Pew Research Center "Limbaugh Holds onto his Niche—Conservative Men" February 3, 2009

feverishly to everyone within earshot about welfare queens, environmental "wackos," "feminazis," and of course, the "liberal media." Senko become a conspiracy theorist, fretting constantly about threats against America, avoiding any disconfirming data, and drowning himself in right-wing email newsletters. He was so vitriolic that his own family came to avoid him.

In his book *Freedom of Mind: Helping Loved Ones Leave Controlling People, Cults, and Beliefs*, brainwashing expert Steven Hassan describes cult tactics with something he calls the BITE Model, which breaks down as follows:[66]

Behavioral control

Information control

Thought control

Emotional control

By carefully shaping the narrative, using loaded language, teaching thought-stopping techniques, stoking divisions, fueling distrust, and claiming to be the only reliable source for truth, cults effectively lock their members into an alternate reality. These cults and cult leaders don't just shape the world, they become the world. They are the reality beyond reality, which often explains the cult-like nature of right-wing radio.

A friend of mine, Steve, was featured in *The Brainwashing of My Dad*. He had once been a dittohead. After I'd seen the film, I called Steve to get more information. Turns out he had voted for Clinton in 1992 and held fairly progressive opinions until he began listening to Rush Limbaugh on his fifty-five-mile commute to work. As the Rush Rage spilled into his car, Steve began to change. In his words,

> The more I listened, the angrier I became. Or maybe the more I listened, the more I channeled the natural anger and

---

66   www.freedomofmind.com/bite-model

frustrations of a young man into a new direction. I was suddenly alarmed at the state of our once-great nation. I could see how our moral fabric was being torn asunder and our freedoms were being eroded before our very eyes. We were surely on a path to ruin, and idiots like me who had voted Democrat had paved that path right over the graves of all the great and noble people who built this country.

Steve finished his thoughts with a sobering line. "I had been brainwashed...by people I'd never even met."

Steve and I were much like Frank Senko: white, male, Republican, and mad at the world. Fortunately, we both escaped the right-wing outrage machine.

Regarding Frank, it was only when his radio broke, his TV channel changed, and his wife unsubscribed him from the conspiracy sites, replacing them with more liberal content, that a "deprogramming" began to take place. His jaw loosened. His heart relaxed. His outlook improved. His world expanded. Soon after, Frank stunned his wife when he declared that he supported gay marriage. In the 2012 presidential election, Frank Senko voted for Obama.

The Fox News Christian, and perhaps my skeptical readers, might be quick to protest that Frank Senko traded one bias for another. It's fair to acknowledge that progressive media informed his shift in attitudes and values. But with Frank, I'm most interested in the transformation in the man. In his post-Rush life, Frank became less prone to anger, more balanced, kinder. His daughter declared "There's finally been peace in our house. My dad is more content than I've ever seen him." The days of rage, paranoia, and division are behind him, and family bonds have been restored.

Yet there are still more than 600 radio stations blasting Rush Limbaugh to tens of millions of people every week, and Rush was recently elevated even higher on the American political ladder.

On Limbaugh's February 3, 2020, radio show, he announced to his listeners that he had been diagnosed with advanced lung cancer. Detractors basked in the irony, as the cigar-smoking host is on record declaring, "There is no conclusive proof that nicotine's addictive" and "the same thing with cigarettes causing emphysema, lung cancer, heart disease."[67] (Talk about fake news.) In the wake of the cancer announcement, at President Trump's 2020 State of the Union address, Rush Limbaugh was awarded America's highest civilian honor, The Presidential Medal of Freedom. Donald Trump lauded Rush's "decades of tireless devotion to our country" and "the millions of people a day that you speak to and inspire."

The moment was historic for all the wrong reasons. A disgraceful radio host who once claimed that AIDS "is the only federally protected virus,"[68] who suggested that actor Michael J. Fox was faking his Parkinson's symptoms,[69] and who told Sean Hannity in 2008 that Barack Obama was "a veritable rookie whose only chance of winning is that he's black"[70] was given the distinction of Great American. In my conservative youth, I might have stood and applauded. Today I'm genuinely discouraged about the people we call heroes.

There's a broader, more beautiful sound beyond the narrow bands of right-wing radio. It's fairer, more reasonable, more optimistic, more compassionate, and more American. It's the sound of a better humanity, and it deserves to be heard.

---

67 Rush Limbaugh radio show April 29, 1994
68 The Most Dangerous Man in America: Rush Limbaugh's Assault on Reason by John K. Wilson 2011
69 Rush Limbaugh radio show October 23, 2006
70 Fox News Hannity January 22, 2009

CHAPTER THREE:

The Reagan Revolution: Christian Nationalism, Communism, and the Cold War

THE OSTENTATIOUS '80S. Globally, it was an exciting decade. The 1980s brought us the personal computer, cable television and home video, cell phones, test-tube babies (in-vitro fertilization), the space shuttle program, hard-won strides forward for women's and LGBT rights, the beginning of the crumbling of the Berlin Wall, and of course, the Internet. It was the time of big hair, big ideas, and big business. It was the time of Ronald Reagan, fortieth president of the United States.

Reagan, the entertainer-as-president precursor to Donald Trump, was a marginally popular movie star in the 1930s and 1940s who became synonymous with the characters he played on-screen, projecting a classic American "good guy" persona that enraptured audiences. Reagan was Knute Rockne, the legendary Notre Dame football coach known as The Gipper (*Knute Rockne, All American* 1940). He was the righteous U.S. marshal who brought The Durango Kid to justice (*Law and Order* 1953). He battled the Japanese as a stalwart WWII submarine commander (*Hellcats of the Navy* 1957). When Reagan was commissioned as a second lieutenant in the Army Reserves, he joined the Army's First Motion Picture Unit and became a public relations dream, narrating military films with titles like *For God and Country*.

The military and the Second World War fueled a change in Reagan's once liberal(ish) worldview. When he left Hollywood for politics in the 1950s, Ronald Reagan quickly positioned himself as a pro-individual, low-tax, small-government opponent of anything resembling socialism. He publicly criticized Medicare[71] and the Food Stamp Program[72] as anti-American, and he famously campaigned for conservative presidential candidate Barry Goldwater on the theme of defeating socialist "totalitarianism."[73]

Reagan's ascendency to governor of California in 1966 was fueled by a distrust of liberal "peaceniks" as the Vietnam War raged (Reagan blasted the campus protesters at UC Berkeley as spoiled and undeserving[74]). In 1969, a year before the famous student massacre at Kent State, Reagan called out the California National Guard to deal with protesters at a Berkeley anti-war rally, declaring, "If it takes a bloodbath, let's get it over with. No more appeasement,"[75] strong language from the square-jawed sheriff keeping law and order.

This flavor of tough talk played well among hand-over-heart conservatives and led in part to Ronald Reagan's presidential victory over Jimmy Carter in 1980. Reagan's platform boiled down to Individual Freedom (endowed by Reagan's personal god), reduced interference by government regulations, and God-and-country nationalism.

At sixty-nine, President Reagan was still the Good Guy leading the Good Guys, and Americans rallied under that banner. Economic recession and wartime cynicism had given way to optimism, justice, and misty-eyed patriotism, much of it rooted in the false notion that

---

71 Recorded announcement for the American Medical Association 1961, Ronald Reagan Presidential Library
72 The New York Times "Food Stamps Program: How It Grew and How Reagan Wants to Cut It Back" April 4, 1981
73 Televised speech "A Time for Choosing" October 27, 1964
74 UC Berkeley News "Ronald Reagan launched political career using the Berkeley campus as a target" June 8, 2004
75 The Battle for People's Park, Berkeley 1969 by Tom Dalzell

the United States was founded to be a Christian nation and—with God on its side—would be rewarded for faithfulness with a greater peace (through strength), global influence, and unprecedented national prosperity. After spending the 1970s on life support, the United States was again breathing free and ready to walk tall. This rehabilitation of the country was called the Reagan Revolution.

Yuppie America cheered the soaring stock market (until it crashed in 1987) and Ronald Reagan's "Make my day" bombast about tax cuts and corporate deregulation as the nation accumulated more debt in eight years than in its entire history. The country had rallied behind an already lionized Reagan after John Hinkley's assassination attempt in 1981, perhaps perceiving his survival as divine destiny. And it waved its free-market finger in the face of evil communism, especially Soviet Russia, a favorite villain of American conservatives. When Reagan told Soviet leader Mikhail Gorbachev to "Tear down this [Berlin] wall," it sent a swell of pride throughout the Land of the Free.

I felt this pride in my bones, not simply because the Berlin Wall was a human rights nightmare of division, suppression, and violence, but also because my godly Christian tribe had called out an ungodly communist tribe. My attitudes were rooted in humanism but adorned in religiosity.

Tribalism has always been part of the human condition, and the 1980s saw two tribal superpowers locked in a terrifying cold war, nuclear missiles at the ready, a crusade narrative set firmly in place by Ronald Reagan's references to the "evil empire." Interestingly, that comment was made in Reagan's 1983 address to the National Association of Evangelicals, revealing that, yes, the Republican Party was in bed with evangelical Christianity long before Donald Trump. The GOP has long been quite effective at marketing itself as the Party of God, and while both Republicans and Democrats have a long history of God-speak, the alignment of politics and divine destiny has largely been a GOP strategy.

In my young mind I held to this idea as axiom. A vote for Republicans marked strength and a return toward God. A vote for Democrats betrayed weakness and the rejection of God, or at the very least, a slippery tolerance for those icky non-Christians and secular humanists.

Christian nationalism bled into the public's notions about the American military. Until 1972, religious services—representing only Christianity, Catholicism, and Judaism—were mandatory in the armed forces. Even today, many mandatory military assemblies begin with prayer. At one point, Jewish army chaplains actually had to petition for their own symbol after the military had embroidered the Latin Cross (representing the crucifixion cross of Jesus Christ) on all chaplain uniforms.[76] Muslims weren't given a crescent uniform symbol until 1993.[77] Various military cemeteries have the Christian cross for their headstones (like Bladensburg, Florida's WWI memorial—a forty-foot cross). In 2010 it was reported that rifle sights manufactured for the U.S. Army bore the engraving 2COR4:6, a reference to the verse in the Christian New Testament that reads, "For God, who commanded the light to shine out of darkness, hath shined in our hearts, to give the light of knowledge of the glory of God in the face of Jesus Christ." And, of course, American evangelicals have long loved their imagery of the U.S. soldier kneeling at the cross under captions like "And God said, 'Let there be Marines,' and the Devil ran in fear."

For God and country. With God on our side. God bless our troops. Even the slogans reflect the American notion of the military as a branch of the Christian religion.

Reagan proudly identified as a born-again Christian, which was common for an American politician, but his outward faith was demonstrated with such zeal that it swept America off its feet. Where Reagan's predecessor, Jimmy Carter, reflected a more pessimistic, oppressed era still reeling from Vietnam and Watergate, Ronald Reagan puffed

---

76 The Fighting Rabbis: Jewish Military Chaplains and American History Albert Slomovitz 1999
77 Encyclopedia of the United States Army Insignia and Uniforms University of Oklahoma 1996

---

the fresh air of optimism, confidence, and pride—a pride that seemed to insulate him, even in scandal.

American Republicans saluted Oliver North, the Vietnam war veteran and National Security Staff member involved in the weapons-for-hostages Iran Contra scandal, as a hero. North ultimately segued from scandal to senator to president of the National Rifle Association. From 2001 to 2016, North also hosted a television show called *War Stories with Oliver North*. The network? Fox News.

At the time, Oliver North seemed to reflect Ronald Reagan's view of the United States as the white knight crusading against communism. In 1986, when government officials secretly facilitated the sale of weapons to Iran during an arms embargo to fund the anti-communist and U.S.-backed Contra rebels in Nicaragua, the scheme blew up in their faces, leaving Oliver North and Ronald Reagan scrambling.

I was still a teenager in 1986. I knew nothing about Iran, communism, or Contras. But somehow I knew—deep in my bones—that President Reagan and Oliver North were acting for the cause of good, an antidote to the poison of Satan's communism, righteous defenders of One Nation Under God. My religion and culture had conditioned me to filter world events through the lens of Christianity and Republican talking points, so no further research was necessary. I felt a rush of pride as Lieutenant Colonel Oliver North gave testimony during the 1987 Iran-Contra hearings. The phenomenon of Olliemania swept conservative circles, with tens of millions tuning in to the televised proceedings. Even as North admitted to lying, shredding documents, and falsifying records to protect senior White House officials, any ugly admissions were overshadowed by the visual of the proud, Marine-uniformed patriot battling communism.

Not yet twenty years old, I was already parroting and voting the religious and political bias of my tribe, neatly stacking the hugely convoluted and complex world into two convenient piles: Right versus Left. Republican versus Democrat. Straight versus gay. Capitalist versus

Communist. American versus foreigner. Christian versus non-Christian. Good versus evil.

On March 8, 1983, President Reagan said the following in his speech to the National Association of Evangelicals:

> I believe that communism is another sad, bizarre chapter in human history whose last pages even now are being written. I believe this because the source of our strength in the quest for human freedom is not material but spiritual. And because it knows no limitation, it must terrify and ultimately triumph over those who would enslave their fellow man.

I'm not selling communism. Rather, I'm trying to describe how a political theory had been culturally linked to claims of supernatural dark forces and a Christian Nation narrative. In fact, almost every political position seemed to carry religious baggage, as reflected in Ronald Reagan's early tirades against government social programs such as welfare. Certainly government assistance can be and often has been abused by those gaming the system, but in my young Republican brain, I echoed Ronald Reagan's 1960s political mantra, "Send the welfare bums back to work; God helps those who help themselves." In my conspicuously coddled, insulated, white, middle-class, Christian viewpoint, those living on handouts probably weren't diligent or driven enough to warrant God's favor, and failure was ultimately their own fault.

I'm embarrassed by my cruelty of attitude toward those who'd had the deck stacked against them from birth. I'd never been racially profiled or denied a job because of my gender or skin color. I'd never gone hungry because of poverty. I'd never been ostracized over my person, politics, or philosophies. And I had gorged myself at the table of white Christian privilege while so many others suffered a famine of fairness.

Whether or not you support identity politics, there can be no doubt that the United States is a country that long oppressed and suppressed its minorities while the privileged blamed the downtrodden for their own misery. This was certainly true in my case. I'd bought the conservative party line that promised the American Dream to anyone and everyone who wanted it, and I squinted through my tiny Oklahoma window at the non-white, the non-American, the non-Christian, the Other.

Fears about the Other fueled Reagan's tragic fumbling of the AIDS crisis, which began in the 1980s and was considered by many evangelicals to be a "gay plague."[78] Again the religious Right was cramming a global health problem into its moral cookie cutter. In my circles it was often claimed that AIDS was a divine punishment for aberrant sexual behavior, with God unleashing the sickness as he did to the Old Testament Egyptians during the rebellion of Pharaoh. From that high mountain, evangelicals could divorce themselves from the unthinkable grief and suffering wrought by AIDS, planting their Christian flags upon the bodies of the dead. From their high horses the pious sneered. *There are consequences for not doing Christianity.*

This appears to have been the attitude within Ronald Reagan's White House. In Scott Calonico's sobering documentary short, *When AIDS Was Funny*, never-before-heard audio tapes reveal a frightening callousness among Reagan staffers. The film contains a 1982 recording of Press Secretary Larry Speakes dismissing journalist Lester Kinsolving with deflections and chuckles, with much of the press corps joining in.

AIDS was a largely unknown animal in the 1980s, and cultural ignorance fueled national ambivalence. The disease was largely perceived as a "gay problem." Evangelicals and others often refused handshakes and hugs with non-heterosexuals, deriding AIDS victims as bathhouse scoundrels paying the fatal price for their perversity. At the very least, many evangelicals remained initially untouched and unmoved by a condition that devastated the lives of "the homos," their indifference adorned in piety, their pastors pounding the pulpits of indignation over sin, their leaders—including Reagan—conveniently silent about

---

78   Documentary short: When AIDS Was Funny, director Scott Calonico

this twentieth-century plague.

In fact Ronald Reagan himself said nothing—not one word—about the AIDS epidemic until 1985. By that time, more than 5,000 people, mostly gay men, were already dead.[79] That same year, the Reagan administration recommended a $10 million cut in AIDS spending from its federal budget, despite the protestations of the National Cancer Institute's Dr. Robert Gallo (who arguably discovered the virus) that the government's response was "not nearly enough."[80]

Only in the seventh year of his presidency did Reagan give a speech about AIDS. It was May 31, 1987. The president had apparently been moved by the death of longtime friend and film star Rock Hudson, a Hollywood leading man of the 1960s who had recently died of AIDS-related complications, and at the request of Hudson's friend and costar Elizabeth Taylor (National Chairperson of the American Foundation for AIDS Research), Reagan addressed a full house at AMFAR. At this event he finally spoke to the devastation wrought by the disease and against the public phobias surrounding it. He pledged more money for AIDS research. He lauded the development of the treatment drug AZT. He discouraged panic and spoke words of compassion, with one interesting caveat. Reagan's speech included this statement:

> What our citizens must know is this: America faces a disease that is fatal and spreading. And this calls for urgency, not panic. It calls for compassion, not blame. And it calls for understanding, not ignorance. It's also important that America not reject those who have the disease, but care for them with dignity and kindness. *Final judgment is up to God* [emphasis mine]; our part is to ease the suffering and to find a cure.

Seeded within a rousing call to respect, dignity, and empathy was this curious reference to God and judgment. I'm convinced it was a riff on Christianity's popular motto, "Hate the sin, love the sinner." Certainly

---

79   Vanity Fair "The Reagan Administration's Unearthed Response to the AIDS Crisis is Chilling" December 1, 2015

80   The New York Times "Reagan Defends Financing for AIDS" September 18, 1985

Ronald Reagan should be given some kind of credit for finally landing on the side of compassion and support, but why would his speech to AMFAR include references to HIV babies, IV drug users, and hemophiliacs but totally omit the vast gay population most devastated by the disease? (More than 40,000 people died of AIDS in 1987, most of them gay men.[81]) And why would a speech about compassion also include the line about judgment in the eyes of God unless there was an underlying subtext about the morally dubious Other? Was a benevolent Reagan politically savvy enough to pander to his base with a reference to the Judgment Seat? Was he craftily assuaging the moral panic of Christian fundamentalists who were terrified of the LGBT community? Did he wrestle against his own Disciples of Christ upbringing in the face of human suffering? It's impossible to know for sure.

What we do know is that the six critical, precious years between the discovery of AIDS and Reagan's AMFAR speech were tragic and costly. Ronald Reagan had closed the stable doors long after the horses had bolted, and the United States lost precious time as the Reagan White House sat uncomfortably on its hands. Certainly it was a time of cultural ignorance and some understandable fears, but the puritanism of homophobic Christians undoubtedly made a horrific problem worse, and Ronald Reagan had arrived unfashionably late to a critical human rights party. This didn't and doesn't look good.

Reagan's supporters largely looked like him. In fact, two-thirds of white evangelical voters voted for Reagan in the 1980 election.[82] It mattered little that Reagan was little more than a cultural Christian, rarely attending church and on his second marriage. The evangelical Right needed a champion, and Reagan's election almost immediately saw religious organizations like Reverend Jerry Falwell's Moral Majority swoop in to dance across the constitutional state/church line. Falwell wrapped Christian privilege and anti-gay bigotry in the

---

81 And the Band Played On: Politics, People, and the AIDS Epidemic by Randy Shilts 1987

82 The New York Times "Religion and Right-Wing Politics: How Evangelicals Shaped Elections" October 28, 2018

---

hollow language of "traditional values." Reagan glad-handed with Jerry Falwell at events like the 1984 National Religious Broadcasters convention, having recently proclaimed 1983 The Year of the Bible.[83]

Attorney and activist Phyllis Schlafly, founder of the conservative political interest group Eagle Forum and dubbed The First Lady of American Conservatism, was vehemently opposed to abortion, same-sex marriage, and the feminist movement on moral and biblical grounds. Reagan sent a personalized message of thanks to Phyllis Schlafly and attendees of Eagle Forum in 1984, invoking his "Creator" and reaffirming his conviction that (Christian) prayer belonged in public schools.[84] Reagan reiterated this call for prayer in schools on the Christian Broadcasting Network's *700 Club* in September 1985, telling host Pat Robertson, "I am convinced that this is one nation under God."

From the early days of Reagan's first presidential campaign, his appeal to evangelicals was front and center even as he addressed the students at Bob Jones University in 1980. Jones, a young-Earth Creationist, had founded the fundamentalist Christian college in 1927 amid fears about the teaching of evolution in schools and the growing secularization of America. True to its notions of "traditional values," BJU didn't allow black students until 1971. University policy forbade interracial dating and marriage until the year 2000, when it finally issued an official apology for having allowed "institutional policies to remain in place that were racially hurtful."[85] The racism of Bob Jones University nevertheless was still fully on display during Reagan's road to the White House, with Ronald Reagan seemingly ignorant or unconcerned about BJU's prejudicial policies.

Time and again, by both purpose and accident, the ostensibly holy marriage of white Christianity and American politics was consecrated, and evangelicals rejoiced. I rejoiced with them.

---

83   "Remarks at the Annual Convention of National Religious Broadcasters," Ronald Reagan Presidential Library
84   Ronald Reagan's Message to Phyllis Schlafly and Eagle Council 1984
85   "Bob Jones Univ. Apologizes for Racist Policies" NBC News November 21, 2008

The Reagan Era resisted social change and was a pep rally for American evangelicals who felt validated and emboldened. As conservative columnist Cal Thomas said, "It was, like, come up out of the catacombs—you know, you don't have to be silent anymore."[86] After decades of political impotence, Christian nationalists finally had their champion.

Ronald Reagan remained hugely popular until he left office in 1989, his conservative mantle passed to George H. W. Bush. The late 1980s remained a time of national optimism. The reunification of Germany was happening. The Cold War was waning. The Soviet Union would soon fall.

Bush's Episcopalian religion was front and center in his presidency. His inaugural address included a prayer, and he mentioned prayer in two hundred speeches and remarks during his presidential tenure.[87] Bush is credited with moving the Republican party further to the right on issues such as birth control, female reproductive choice, and stem cell or fetal tissue advancements to help fight disease. This resistance to science and reproductive autonomy continues today, and it has found renewed vigor in the Donald Trump era.

George H. W. Bush managed only one term before the political pendulum swung back toward the left, but Christian nationalist citizens and organizations had used the previous decade to embed themselves back into the American Republican identity. The GOP wasn't just conservative. It was the Party of God.

Ronald Reagan had laid the foundation on which theocrats could built their church, and for American conservatives, that church would be the government of the United States.

---

86   The New York Times "Religion and Right-Wing Politics: How Evangelicals Shaped Elections" October 28, 2018
87   Faith and the Presidency from George Washington to George W. Bush by Gary Scott Smith 2009

CHAPTER FOUR:

A Pledge of Allegiance: Loyalty Oaths and the Freedom of Speech

THE CAMBRIDGE DICTIONARY defines *allegiance* as "support for a leader, country, group, or belief." Merriam-Webster calls it "the fidelity owed by a subject or citizen to a sovereign or government."

The more benign Cambridge definition seems to align with the best notions of patriotism, with the verb *support* open to all kinds of interpretation. After all, someone can support its country's constitution while criticizing its leaders and their actions. Many of our recent history's greatest patriots were often also its most vocal critics. One of recent history's most famous examples, Martin Luther King, Jr., publicly criticized American racism, poverty, class oppression, and the Vietnam War, not because he hated America, but "because I love her. I want her to stand as a moral example to the world."

Of course, my idealistic younger self—the Fox News Christian—held to the Merriam-Webster model, which framed allegiance as a kind of feudal bond between an American and his country. This allegiance was cemented by ritual, drilled early into children's consciousness as they stood before the national flag with hand over heart and repeated a sacred oath:

I pledge allegiance to the flag of the United States of America and to the Republic for which it stands, one nation under God,[88] indivisible, with liberty and justice for all.

From elementary school to Sunday school, from my earliest memories and well into adulthood, I recited the Pledge of Allegiance, yet at no point was I ever encouraged to examine the oath I was taking, to define and understand the words, or to ponder the implications. It wasn't important that eight-year-olds thoughtfully consider the vow they were making. The pledge was simply the reiteration of a grandfathered contract, an exercise in rote recitation that cheated true understanding and avoided questions. *How do you define allegiance?* Not sure. *What's a republic?* No idea. Just straighten up and say the words. The act itself is the important thing.

I'm not saying that reciting the Pledge of Allegiance is always an exercise in cult behavior, but my own religious upbringing framed the pledge in very cultish ways. In my private Christian schools, we recited a series of pledges, beginning with an oath to the United States followed by an oath before the Christian flag and finally to the Bible. In this setting the Pledge of Allegiance itself was not unlike a recitation of the Lord's Prayer, spoken in reverence as part of an overarching religious exercise. My nation was sovereign. It belonged to Christianity. It was constructed upon biblical principles by Christian people. It was a Christian nation. (We'll get to the religious beliefs of the Founding Fathers shortly.)

Even those who recite the Pledge of Allegiance without any overt religious window dressing often do so with an attitude of piety that might feel right at home within the Baptist church, the Muslim mosque, or the Hindu temple.

If I may digress for just a moment, I'll wager that some of my readers are already stiffening at the spine. In their view, we can question prayers in public schools, religious exercises in state and national

---

88   This phrase was added by Congress and President Eisenhower in 1954.

government, laws promoted by theocrats, misrepresentations of the Constitution, and so on. But the Pledge of Allegiance? The noble loyalty oath given by citizens blessed with blood-bought freedoms unknown to much of the modern world? Unthinkable.

This indignant recoil helps to demonstrate how revered the pledge has become in the American consciousness. As United States citizens, we recite the Pledge of Allegiance like Catholics take the sacraments, and those who pause at the ritual risk heresy. I consider this attitude unhealthy, especially in a country continually waxing about freedom. In fact, a genuinely free mind should/would eagerly explore any idea or practice with the goal of determining its merits. The "tradition" argument isn't nearly enough, nor are thought-stopping warnings by the Fox Newsers about the erosion of "American values."[89]

The Fox News morning show *Fox & Friends* held a bizarre segment in 2018 that staged school children in front of desks, their right hands over their hearts, their left hands holding up a small American flag, to recite the Pledge of Allegiance on live television[90] as host Pete Hegseth tweeted that parents and teachers should "demand patriotism in our classrooms."[91] Conservative author and radio host Todd Starnes, a frequent Fox News contributor, has linked the pledge to "traditional American values, God and country" (there's that religious language again).[92] In my home state, Republican Senator Rob Standridge—another Fox guest—proposed a 2013 bill that would require the Pledge of Allegiance to be recited daily in Oklahoma public schools. Standridge framed the pledge as a poignant tribute to the founders and the veterans of American wars. Interestingly, United States senators recite the pledge immediately after a chaplain's prayer. God and country, a one-two punch.

Standridge's narrative, common among political conservatives, has

---

89 Fox News opinion "Todd Starnes: The Pledge of Allegiance Flap Latest Example of the Left's Plan to Eradicate American Values, Traditions" May 3, 2019
90 "Fox & Friends Honors the Pledge of Allegiance" December 28, 2018
91 Twitter @PeteHegseth 9:00am December 28, 2018
92 Fox News opinion "Todd Starnes: Seniors told to Pledge Allegiance to the flag—in a Closet" July 17, 2019

the effect of vilifying Pledge of Allegiance skeptics as desecrators of military graves. If you question the pledge, you're spitting on the veterans who fought for its principles. Spit on our veterans, and you're a traitor to America. (We saw this flavor of indignation recently, when NFL player Colin Kaepernick knelt in protest at the national anthem and received criticism, hate, and even death threats.) This provincialism stands in contrast to the very idea of free speech and personal liberty. Our veterans bled and died so that Americans would be forced to speak specific words at specific times under specific conditions? Wouldn't this notion be more at home within a totalitarian, anti-speech regime like North Korea?

In 2019 activist Cabot Phillips, editor-in-chief of the conservative publication *Campus Reform* (and a Fox News favorite), contrasted pledge opposition by the student government at Michigan's Grand Valley State University against the life-and-death Chinese military siege against human rights activists at Hong Kong's Polytechnic University.[93] From Phillips's perspective, American students' concerns about a mandated, exclusionary pledge was little more than manufactured oppression by social justice warriors choking on their own privilege. These American kids were coddled, ungrateful idealists who took their own fortunes for granted, blissfully far from the tear gas and rubber bullets flying in Hong Kong.

After a massive blowup, the GVSU decided to reinstate the pledge to its meetings a mere week after its removal. I read the statement from GVSU Student Senate President Eric-John Szczepaniak and found it reasonable. He said, "The intent was to help make our meetings as inclusive as possible; we didn't want to 'other' anybody."[94] In short, the student government engaged in a democratic process, originally voting 22 to 10 (the ten abstaining) to remove the required pledge from its meetings to prevent anyone from feeling marginalized by a required oath.

---

93 Fox News opinion "Cabot Phillips" Opposition to Pledge of Allegiance by 'social justice warriors" Signals Alarming Trend" December 7, 2019
94 Michigan Live "GVSU Student Government Reinstates Pledge of Allegiance after Backlash from Students, Parents, Donors" November 19, 2019

Free expression. A democratic vote. This act should have been culturally accepted as an exercise in constitutional liberty. Instead it was crushed in a conservative crusade against desecration. The students had questioned the pledge, spit on the veterans, and behaved like traitors. The heresy scenario played out like clockwork, and the righteous indignation surrounding the GVSU decision prompted a quick reversal by the student government. One could argue that the reversal was informed by the free speech of pledge proponents, but there's little doubt that anti-pledge students were treated like turncoats. Pledgers hadn't simply disagreed with the decision to strike the pledge from meetings and voiced concern; they were calling for the hanging of Judas.

This is dogmatism.

In 2014 the American Humanist Association launched the controversial campaign titled Boycott the Pledge.[95] The AHA's web page for the campaign was fronted with a quote from U.S. Supreme Court Associate Justice Robert Jackson: "If there is any fixed star in our constitutional constellation, it is that no official, high or petty, can prescribe what shall be orthodox in politics, nationalism, religion, or other matters of opinion or force citizens to confess by word or act their faith therein." This quote came out of the June 14, 1944, Supreme Court ruling that compelling children in public schools to salute the U.S. flag was unconstitutional and a violation of their freedom of speech and freedom of religion, and it favored one group of students over another.[96]

Twenty years ago I would have blanched at the AHA's campaign. At that time in my life, I was also still married to the Christian nationalist narrative, so the striking of the "under God" portion of the pledge informed feelings of religious persecution; my god and my country were under attack from within.

---

95   American Humanist Association BoycottThePledge.com
96   West Virginia State Board of Education v. Barnett 1943

For the American Humanist Association, the pledge's religious phrasing was partly the point. Was it right to force non-theist Americans (atheists, agnostics, deists, etc.) to commit their allegiance to God? Wasn't the reference to God exclusionary to the non-religious, rendering them, in effect, second-class citizens? Why was God-speak part of a national oath? Would the Christian "religious liberty" crowd rally to defend the phrasing of "under Allah" or "under Krishna," especially if required to speak the words in a daily ritual?

The AHA's campaign tagline remains *Sit for the Pledge. Stand for the Constitution*, a philosophy that has gotten a great many pledge detractors into trouble. Seventeen-year-old Windfern High School student India Landry was expelled for remaining silent and seated during the pledge, prompting a lawsuit involving the Texas attorney general.[97] In 2019 a first-year student at Manchester High School in Akron, Ohio, was banished to the principal's office for not reciting the oath.[98] The principal of Mira Costa High School in Manhattan Beach, California, actually patrolled the classrooms for pledge defectors, announcing that he was "personally offended by any teacher or student who did not stand for the pledge."[99] Attorney David Niose chronicled the story of "Alicia," a high school sophomore condemned for treason by one of her own teachers.[100] The pledge was sacrosanct. But where had it come from?

The original Pledge of Allegiance was composed in 1892—by a socialist. Francis Bellamy was a devout Baptist minister and Christian Socialist who sought a greater regimentation of society in an equal and classless system.[101] He penned the pledge for a popular children's magazine called *The Youth's Companion* to commemorate the 400th

---

97 Washington Post "A Black Student Refused to Recite the Pledge of Allegiance—Challenging Texas Law Requiring It" September 26, 2018

98 American Humanist Association "Humanist Attorneys Protect Student's Right to Not Say the Pledge." May 14, 2019

99 Appignani Humanist Legal Center "CA School Recognizes Right to Boycott Pledge after Warning" October 3, 2019

100 "The Pledge of Allegiance Must Go: A Daily Loyalty Oath has Become a Toxic, Nationalistic Ritual" David Niose, Salon, February 15, 2016

101 Cato Institute "What's Conservative about the Pledge of Allegiance?" Gene Healy, November 4, 2003

anniversary of Christopher Columbus landing in the New World, and it was eventually woven into the national narrative. Alarmingly, even decades before the Second World War, Bellamy's recommended procedure for the pledge was rather Nazi-esque:

> At a signal from the Principal the pupils, in ordered ranks, hands to the side, face the Flag. Another signal is given; every pupil gives the Flag the military salute—right hand lifted, palm downward, to a line with the forehead and close to it. At the words "to my Flag," the right hand is extended gracefully, palm upward, towards the Flag, and remains in this gesture till the end of the affirmation; whereupon all hands immediately drop to the side. —*The Youth's Companion*, 65 (1892)

U.S. Office of War Information photographer Fenno Jacobs caught this striking image of American schoolchildren performing the "Bellamy Salute" in May 1942.

For obvious reasons, the extended palms surrounding the pledge were declared problematic by an America opposed to Italian fascism and Hitler's Germany (with both nations using similar gestures), and the "Bellamy Salute" was replaced by Congress by the more benign hand-over-heart gesture in December of 1942.[102]

But even then "under God" wasn't yet part of the United States Pledge of Allegiance. The phrase was amended into the pledge by Congress on Flag Day in 1954, backed by the words of Presbyterian President Dwight Eisenhower.

> From this day forward, the millions of our school children will daily proclaim in every city and town, every village and rural schoolhouse, the dedication of our nation and our people to the Almighty. In this way, we are affirming the transcendence of religious faith in America's heritage and future. In this way, we shall constantly strengthen those spiritual weapons which forever will be our country's most powerful resource, in peace or in war.[103]

Remember that this was the time of the Cold War, when the United States and the Soviet Union were locked in a geopolitical contest, with freshly minted nuclear weapons primed and ready. Eisenhower injected his personal religion into the American political landscape to great effect. He became the first president to write and read his own inaugural prayer.[104] He brought the famous evangelist Billy Graham into the White House as a spiritual advisor, established a National Day of Prayer, and launched the country's very first National Prayer Breakfast in 1953, telling an enthusiastic audience of influential attendees that "all free government is firmly founded in a deeply felt religious faith."[105]

President Eisenhower often contrasted godly American freedom against godless communist oppression. As he believed that individual rights were endowed by the Creator, and as the Soviet Union and

---

102 United States Flag Code, Public Law 77-623; chapter 435
103 Statement by the president upon signing bill to include the words "Under God" in the Pledge to the Flag, June 14, 1954
104 PBS American Experience "God in the White house"
105 Smithsonian Magazine "The History of the National Prayer Breakfast" February 2, 2017

Mao's communist China stripped away the individual rights in favor of The State, the very notion of communism seemed blasphemous. In a famous radio address in 1954, the same year as the pledge amendment, Eisenhower declared, "Out of faith in God, and through faith in themselves and His children, our forefathers designed and built the Republic." God built the United States, and God governs its principles. Eisenhower saw great utility in framing this political standoff as holy war, and the Pledge of Allegiance served as an affirmation of American godliness over godless communism.

At the time the pledge was codified, a paranoid America was panicked about the infestation of Satan's communist spies. These public fears fueled Senator Joseph McCarthy's House Committee on Un-American Activities, which investigated accusations of communist activity through subpoenas, show trials, and blacklists. McCarthy reigned terror on all who were accused of communist affiliation, warning that "this is the era of Armageddon,"[106] and his domestic holy war, waged within U.S. borders, ruined many lives. Anti-communists marched with signs declaring *The Only Good Communist Is a Dead Communist* and *Better Dead Than Red*. In the Communist Control Act of 1954, Congress declared that communism wasn't a political party, but rather an extension of a "hostile foreign power" and a "continuing danger to the security of the United States."[107] This act had been preceded by President Truman's 1947 Executive Order 9835, known as the Loyalty Order, which required that all federal employees be proven sufficiently allegiant to the U.S. government. In 1951 (Dennis v. United States) the Supreme Court ruled to restrict the free-speech rights of communists.

The Red Scare was a twentieth-century crusade to expose and punish communist witches. The United States was the church; the pledge was a public profession of faith. As such, the pledge became a shield by which people could protect themselves from suspicion. It was also an affirmation of superiority by the pious and a de facto loyalty test that all non-participants failed.

---

106 The Founding Myth: Why Christian Nationalism is Un-American Andrew L. Seidel
107 Communist Control Act 68 Stat. 775, 50 U.S.C. 841-844

The Christian Nation narrative swelled further. In 1955 President Eisenhower signed a bill that required the words "In God We Trust" be printed on all American currency. We were already printing the phrase on most U.S. coins after a post-Civil War religious resurgence. The 1955 bill was cosponsored by Congressman Charles Bennett, who told the House of Representatives that the United States "was founded in a spiritual atmosphere and with a firm trust in God."[108]

I'd been indoctrinated to affirm Bennet's claim that our Founding Fathers were Christians and that the United States was a Christian nation. I'd long painted Crayola portraits of George Washington, John Adams, Benjamin Franklin, Thomas Jefferson, Alexander Hamilton, and James Madison as the champions of my personal faith, their Constitution (which I hadn't actually read) an affirmation of my god. This felt right. After all, why would I challenge my own religious privilege and elevated moral status? Why upset the apple cart when I was enjoying the apples?

I carried this smug presumption well into my young adult life, and my trusted source for political truth—Fox News—was right there to affirm me. Bill O'Reilly often railed against the secularists attacking our religious heritage, his talking points about the "war on Christmas" arriving like clockwork every December. *The O'Reilly Factor* featured guests such as Jon Meacham, author of *American Gospel: God, the Founding Fathers, and the Making of a Nation*, who declared the founders as men of "intense" faith.[109] When President Barack Obama, a Christian, told the president of Turkey in 2009 that we "do not consider ourselves a Christian nation or a Jewish nation or a Muslim nation; we consider ourselves a nation of citizens who are bound by ideals and a set of values," he was blasted by Fox News host Sean Hannity, *America's Newsroom* co-host Megan Kelley, frequent Fox contributor Karl Rove, and Fox News analyst Newt Gingrich, who

---

108 History, Art & Archives: United States House of Representatives "The Legislation Placing 'In God We Trust' on National Currency" July 11, 1955
109 Fox News "The Founding Fathers and the Christian Tradition" The O'Reilly Factor April 11, 2006

protested that the United States is "not a secular country."[110]

Christian nationalists such as Gingrich like to claim that the phrase "so help me God" in political oaths and American courts demonstrate America's ties to the almighty, yet constitutional attorney Andrew Seidel's book, *The Founding Myth: Why Christian Nationalism is Un-American* (required reading, in my opinion) reveals that the phrase "so help me God" was historically little more than etiquette and protocol, even in secular oaths. Seidel also notes the absence of "so help me God" in the U.S. Constitution's instruction on the presidential oath[111] and from the April 30, 1789, induction of George Washington into the White House. The actual religious beliefs of George Washington are largely unknown. Instead of invoking the Christian god, Washington often relied on more deistic references to "Author of the Universe"[112] and today remains a mystery on the religion question.[113]

What about the other founders?

Thomas Jefferson famously wrote John Adams a letter containing this sentiment: "When once we quit the basis of sensation, all is in the wind. To talk of *immaterial* existences is to talk of *nothings*. To say that the human soul, angels, god, are immaterial, is to say they are *nothings*, or that there is no god, no angels, no soul. I cannot reason otherwise; but I believe I am supported in my creed of materialism by Locke, Tracy, and Stewart."[114]

Jefferson did hold to a deistic prime mover that ordered the universe, but his belief certainly wasn't tethered to Christianity. Jefferson saw Jesus as a moral teacher, not as a god-man, and he famously used a razor and scissors to slice all of Christ's miracles out of the Bible. The

---

110 Media Matters "Fox News Figures Outraged Over Obama's 'Christian Nation' Comment" April 9, 2009
111 U.S. Constitution Article 2, Section 1
112 George Washington letter to Harvard College president Reverend Samuel Landon 1789
113 Smithsonian Magazine "Why No One Can Agree on What George Washington Thought about the Relationship Between Church and State" June 12, 2019
114 Letter from Thomas Jefferson to John Adams August 15, 1820, Founders Online National Archives

Jefferson Bible is still on public display at the Smithsonian National Museum of American History. (This sacrilege is ignored by Christian nationalists eager to claim Jefferson as one of their own.) Thomas Jefferson's famous 1802 letter to the Danbury Baptists declared that "religion is a matter that lies solely between a Man and his God," and Jefferson specifically supported "a wall of separation between Church & State."[115]

Would Thomas Jefferson have said the Pledge of Allegiance? Possibly. Would he—as a champion of personal liberty—have mandated it to all citizens? That's certainly not a given. Would Jefferson have said or required the words "under God" as part of the national loyalty oath? I can't imagine so.

The year 1796 saw the signing of a treaty between the United States and Tripoli (now known as Libya) to secure commercial shipping rights and protect American ships from piracy on the Barbary Coast. In this new alliance, the United States sought to reassure Tripoli's Muslims that it wasn't interested in reenacting the Christian occupation of the Crusades, going so far as to include this statement:

> As the Government of the United States of America is **not, in any sense, founded on the Christian religion** (emphasis mine); as it has in itself no character of enmity against the laws, religion, or tranquility of Mussulmen (Muslims); and as the said States never entered into any war or act of hostility against any Mahometan nation, it is declared by the parties that no pretext arising from religious opinions shall ever produce an interruption of the harmony existing between the two countries.—Article 11, Treaty of Tripoli, endorsed by President John Adams

The message couldn't be clearer. The United States respects the right to a religious belief at home and abroad, but it is not a Christian nation.

---

115 Jefferson's Letter to the Danbury Baptists January 1, 1802, Library of Congress,

TRIPOLI.

COMMUNICATED TO THE SENATE, MAY 26, 1797.

UNITED STATES, *May* 26, 1797.

Gentlemen of the Senate:

I lay before you, for your consideration and advice, a treaty of perpetual peace and friendship between the United States of America and the Bey and subjects of Tripoli, of Barbary, concluded, at Tripoli, on the 4th day of November, 1796.

JOHN ADAMS.

Treaty of peace and friendship between the United States of America and the Bey and Subjects of Tripoli, of Barbary.

ARTICLE 1. There is a firm and perpetual peace and friendship between the United States of America and the Bey and subjects of Tripoli, of Barbary, made by the free consent of both parties, and guarantied by the most potent Dey and Regency of Algiers.

ART. 2. If any goods belonging to any nation, with which either of the parties is at war, shall be loaded on board of vessels belonging to the other party, they shall pass free, and no attempt shall be made to take or detain them.

ART. 3. If any citizens, subjects, or effects, belonging to either party, shall be found on board a prize vessel, taken from an enemy by the other party, such citizens or subjects shall be set at liberty, and the effects restored to the owners.

ART. 4. Proper passports are to be given to all vessels of both parties, by which they are to be known. And considering the distance between the two countries, eighteen months, from the date of this treaty, shall be allowed for procuring such passports. During this interval the other papers, belonging to such vessels, shall be sufficient for their protection.

ART. 5. A citizen or subject of either party having bought a prize vessel, condemned by the other party, or by any other nation, the certificates of condemnation and bill of sale shall be a sufficient passport for such vessel for one year; this being a reasonable time for her to procure a proper passport.

ART. 6. Vessels of either party, putting into the ports of the other, and having need of provisions or other supplies, they shall be furnished at the market price. And if any such vessel shall so put in, from a disaster at sea, and have occasion to repair, she shall be at liberty to land and re-embark her cargo without paying any duties. But in no case shall she be compelled to land her cargo.

ART. 7. Should a vessel of either party be cast on the shore of the other, all proper assistance shall be given to her and her people; no pillage shall be allowed; the property shall remain at the disposition of the owners; and the crew protected and succored till they can be sent to their country.

ART. 8. If a vessel of either party should be attacked by an enemy, within gun-shot of the forts of the other, she shall be defended as much as possible. If she be in port she shall not be seized on, or attacked, when it is in the power of the other party to protect her. And when she proceeds to sea, no enemy shall be allowed to pursue her from the same port, within twenty-four hours after her departure.

ART. 9. The commerce between the United States and Tripoli; the protection to be given to merchants, masters of vessels, and seamen; the reciprocal right of establishing consuls in each country; and the privileges, immunities, and jurisdictions, to be enjoyed by such consuls, are declared to be on the same footing with those of the most favored nationsre spectively.

ART. 10. The money and presents demanded by the Bey of Tripoli, as a full and satisfactory consideration on his part, and on the part of his subjects, for this treaty of perpetual peace and friendship, are acknowledged to have been received by him previous to his signing the same, according to a receipt which is hereto annexed, except such part as is promised, on the part of the United States, to be delivered and paid by them on the arrival of their consul in Tripoli; of which part a note is likewise hereto annexed. And no pretence of any periodical tribute or further payments is ever to be made by either party.

ART. 11. As the Government of the United States of America is not, in any sense, founded on the Christian religion; as it has in itself no character of enmity against the laws, religion, or tranquillity, of Mussulmen; and, as the said States never entered into any war, or act of hostility against any Mahometan nation, it is declared by the parties, that no pretext, arrising from religious opinions, shall ever produce an interruption of the harmony existing between the two countries.

ART. 12. In case of any dispute, arising from a violation of any of the articles of this treaty, no appeal shall be made to arms; nor shall war be declared on any pretext whatever. But if the consul, residing at the place where the dispute shall happen, shall not be able to settle the same, an amicable reference shall be made to the mutual friend of the parties, the Dey of Algiers; the parties hereby engaging to abide by his decision. And he, by virtue of his signature to this treaty, engages for himself and successors to declare the justice of the case, according to the true interpretation of the treaty, and to use all the means in his power to enforce the observance of the same.

Signed and sealed at Tripoli, of Barbary, the 3d day of Junad, in the year of the Hegira 1211—corresponding with the 4th day of November, 1796, by

JUSSOF BASHAW MAHOMET, *Bey.*
MAMET, *Treasurer.*
AMET, *Minister of Marine.*
SOLIMAN KAYA.
GALEL, *General of the Troops.*
MAHOMET, *Commander of the City.*
AMET, *Chamberlain.*
ALLY, *Chief of the Divan.*
MAMET, *Secretary.*

Signed and sealed at Algiers, the 4th day of Argill, 1211—corresponding with the 3d day of January, 1797, by

HASSAN BASHAW, *Dey,*

And by the agent Plenipotentiary of the United States of America,

JOEL BARLOW.

It's important to remember that the founders came to this continent fleeing state and church overreach, something they did not want repeated in the American experiment. James Madison opposed a 1785 bill establishing special provision for teaching Christianity in taxpayer-funded schools, calling the idea a "dangerous abuse of power" because religion "can be directed only by reason and conviction, not by force or violence."[116] Would James Madison have mandated the Pledge of Allegiance "under God?"

Thomas Paine, much like Thomas Jefferson, often referenced God as a deistic First Cause, not an involved personal savior, and certainly not the Christian god. In his series of pamphlets published from 1794 to 1807, Paine strongly attacked the institution of the church and organized religion, called Christianity a fable, and declared that "the study of theology, as it stands in Christian churches, is the study of nothing; it is founded on nothing; it rests on no principles; it proceeds by no authorities; it has no data; it can demonstrate nothing; and it admits of no conclusion."[117] Would Thomas Paine have required the pledge, especially one mandated by Christian nationalists?

Benjamin Franklin was a believer, but not necessarily in Jesus Christ as God, with Franklin admitting he had "some doubts to his divinity."[118] In his life Franklin had written parodies about Puritan intolerance and was instead interested in promoting human goodness, observing that "vital religion has always suffered when orthodoxy is more regarded than virtue."[119] Would Franklin have considered a mandated pledge orthodoxy?

The above examples reveal just a few of the complex and nuanced perspectives of the Founding Fathers, but it's clear that the Founders fashioned a Constitution free of religious tests[120] and often rejected religion wholesale. They didn't mention God in the Constitution, and

---

116 Memorial and Remonstrance Against Religious Assessments, James Madison 1785
117 Thomas Paine "The Age of Reason" Part II, Section 21
118 "To Ezra Stiles, With a Statement of His Religious Creed," Benjamin Franklin March 9, 1790
119 The First American: The Life and Times of Benjamin Franklin H.W. Brands 2002
120 U.S. Constitution Article VI, Clause 3

the only mentions of religion serve to keep the government and the church separate.

> Congress shall make no law respecting an establishment of religion, or prohibiting the free exercise thereof; or abridging the freedom of speech, or of the press; or the right of the people peaceably to assemble, and to petition the government for a redress of grievances. —United States Constitution, Amendment 1

> But no religious test shall ever be required as a qualification to any office or public trust under the United States. —United States Constitution, Article VI

This wall of separation was affirmed by the United States Supreme Court in 1947, with Justice Hugo Black affirming, "No person can be punished for entertaining or professing religious beliefs or disbeliefs."[121] In a statement for the majority opinion, Justice Black repeated Thomas Jefferson's reference to "a wall of separation between church and state." The famous 1963 case of Abington Township v. Schempp saw the Supreme Court strike down mandatory classroom recitations of The Lord's Prayer and school-sponsored Bible reading as unconstitutional because those practices, in the context of taxpayer-funded education, offended the First Amendment.[122] In my home state of Oklahoma, the state Supreme Court ruled in 2014 that a Ten Commandments monument on state capitol grounds was unconstitutional because it promoted religion with public money.[123] At the time of this writing, a similar capitol monument in Arkansas is being challenged in the courts.

Yet Christian nationalists continue to push religion in violation of the Constitution, and because they've so often been rightly swatted down on state/church grounds, the evangelicals changed their tactics. They adopted the narrative that (wait for it) "under God" and "In God We

---

121 U.S. Supreme Court ruling, Everson v. Board of Education (New Jersey) 1947
122 U.S. Supreme Court ruling, Abington School District v. Schempp 1963
123 Oklahoma Supreme Court ruling, Prescott v. Capitol Preservation Commission 2014

Trust" don't constitute religious language. In 1970, the United States Court of Appeals for the Ninth Circuit heard the case of Stefan Ray Aronow, who wanted to strike "In God We Trust" from U.S. currency, and the court ruled that the phrase is "of patriotic or ceremonial character and bears no true resemblance to a governmental sponsorship or a religious exercise."[124] In other words, it's not religion. It's *tradition*.

A trust/loyalty statement toward God is not religious? I thought that trust in God was the whole point. It certainly was when the pledge amendment and new national motto were implemented in the 1950s, and when America's high-profile pastors are being honest, it's the driving agenda behind their defenses of "under God." Yet the tradition-not-religion lie has been an effective strategy for breaching the state/church wall, as seen in the 2004 U.S. Supreme Court ruling about "In God We Trust" on coinage, with Justice Sandra Day O'Connor declaring that the phrase is no longer religious in nature but is instead "ceremonial deism,"[125] a historical artifact woven into the American national culture. By the way, the term "ceremonial deism" makes no logical sense. Deism is the belief in a nameless and unknown supreme being, a prime mover that created the universe but does not intervene in the lives of human beings, so trusting in an uninvolved, deistic god would be an exercise in futility.

When I was a Christian, I would have been disgusted by any attempts to divorce the god in the pledge from the personal god of my religion. The United States was God's house, and all other religions (and those icky atheists) were banished to the cheap seats. My perspective was informed by the attitudes of my family and culture, and their attitudes were informed by the religious rhetoric, moral superiority, xenophobia, and Christian nationalist worldviews born of the Eisenhower era. But those attitudes were not the attitudes of the Founding Fathers. Those attitudes aren't represented in the founding documents. Those attitudes don't align with the protections of free speech and personal liberty.

---

124 U.S. Court of Appeals Ninth Circuit, Aronow v. United States October 6, 1970
125 The term first used in the Supreme Court opinion in Lynch v. Donnelly 1984

Those attitudes are un-American.

I've drifted a bit from the original focus of this chapter—the pledge—to provide framework, but all these religious references tie together. They reveal a paranoid and superstitious chapter in American history, one that overcompensated for its fears about the Other with sermons about national destiny and biblical morality, sermons as dogmatic as the loyalty oath of Hitler's Germany: "I swear: I will be faithful and obedient to the leader of the German Reich and people, Adolf Hitler, to observe the law, and to conscientiously fulfill my official duties, so help me God."

I'm not opposed to a loyalty oath in its ideal form—a promise not to break trust with one's nation or act in bad faith against it. In that context, those enjoying the Constitutional rights, opportunities, and protections provided by the United States would effectively be promising not to bite the hand that feeds them. The pledge could act as a social contract between citizen and nation, not in a dogmatic way but as an assurance of honorable behavior.

Yet even that utopian notion of the pledge would not be a religious exercise. It wouldn't mandate religious language, and it wouldn't be culturally foisted on those who didn't want to participate. There would be no shaming, shunning, hostility, sermonizing, or lawsuits, and the sons and daughters of liberty wouldn't be forced to echo the words of a nineteenth-century socialist whose model for loyalty included Marxist notions about Christ and military-style salutes.

If we could only evolve our ideas about the Pledge of Allegiance to include those who choose not to recite it, American free expression would be—genuinely—free.

CHAPTER FIVE:

We're Number One: National Pride and American Exceptionalism

Dramatized conversation overheard at a party

"The United States is the greatest nation on the face of the Earth."
"Really? What makes it great?"
"Freedom."

"Other nations don't have freedom?"
"Not like America does."
"What's the difference?"
"Soldiers died for our freedom."
"Haven't the soldiers of other nations done the same?"

"We have free speech."
"So does all of Europe."
"And freedom of the press."
"So does Latin America."
"And freedom of religion."
"So does Canada."

"We have a strong military."
"So do Russia and China."
"We're innovative."

"So is Japan."

"We have fewer crimes."

"We have more than New Zealand."

"We have an affordable cost of living."

"Ours is higher than Italy and Germany."

(pause)

"We're still the greatest country."

"Why?"

"Because we are!"

Welcome to the psyche of a common heartland nationalist.

Staunch American conservatives often plant their victory flags on ground they claim is higher than all others. Nationalists are tribalists. They're like the fans of a playoff team chanting, "We've got spirit; yes, we do. We've got spirit; how about you?" Even if the game results in defeat, there are hugs and high fives as coaches and fans assure the home team that "you're still a winner in my book."

In General George Patton's famous speech to the United States Third Army in 1944, he said the classic line, "Americans love a winner and will not tolerate a loser." Patton went on to boast that "Americans have never lost and will never lose a war," a claim soon proven false in the jungles of Vietnam. But Patton's language reflects many American notions of righteous power. Patton was gruff, tough, and often nasty. He saluted his flag, spoke lyrically about honor, and detested weakness, infamously slapping two shell-shocked Army soldiers after assuming them cowards. (Patton didn't believe in PTSD.) When the general rolled his army across the Rhine River in Nazi Germany, he was photographed urinating in the waters. The winner pisses on the losers.

Many hawkish Republicans and old-school conservatives revere George Patton, and I think their attitudes explain much about the popularity of President Donald Trump. Trump famously received no fewer than five military deferments during the Vietnam War, one for an alleged diagnosis of bone spurs; the others for education, but there's no doubt he has long applied a crush-your-enemies philosophy in the business and political world. Trump has long divided people into two basic camps: weak and strong. Hundreds of presidential statements bear this fact out as he blasts his enemies—real or perceived—with insults like "loser," "dumb," "weak," and "pathetic."[126] Here are a few of Trump's own words:

- "[Vietnam veteran and former POW John McCain] has been losing so long he doesn't know how to win anymore." — Twitter, February 9, 2017

- "[Joe Biden] is weak, both mentally and physically." —Twitter, March 22, 2018

- "[Trump's former lawyer Michael Cohen] is a weak person and a not very smart person.",—White House Lawn Press Conference, November 29, 2018

- "[Democratic Representatives Rashida Tlaib, Ilhan Omar, Alexandra Ocasio-Cortez, and Ayanna Pressley] are weak & insecure people..." —Twitter, July 21, 2019

- "[Golden State Warriors Coach and Trump critic Steve Kerr] looks weak and pathetic." —Twitter, October 11, 2019

Trump policies are strong. Past policies were weak. Trump's appointees are solid. Critics are unstable. Trump's stature looms. Political opponents are diminutive. This projection of largeness and strength is so important to Donald Trump that he has ridiculed political opponents for not being physically tall enough. In a February 2, 2020, Fox News interview with Sean Hannity, Trump mocked billionaire Democratic presidential candidate Mike Bloomberg, who stands five feet eight inches tall, for being "very little."

---

126 Newsweek "Stupid, Incompetent, Racist, Loser: Do Trump's Tweets Project His Own Faults into Others?" 6-17-19

Even Donald Trump's dissonant comments about North Korea's murderous dictator Kim Jong Un reveal big-man bravado. In one breath Trump threatens "fire and fury like the world has never seen"[127] against a cartoonish "Rocket Man,"[128] and in the next breath he tells Sean Hannity that Kim is "a real personality. He's very smart, and he's a real leader. He likes me, I like him."[129] At a Trump-Kim February 2019 summit in Singapore, Trump called the dictator "a great leader." Kim Jong Un ticks many of Trump's boxes for greatness. Kim answers to no one. His word is absolute. He's the king of his lands. He crushes all opposition. Donald Trump admires these things.

Defenders are quick to explain that Donald Trump is strategically flattering his way toward the neutralization of a foreign threat, attracting flies with honey, but his schizophrenic tweetstorms don't affirm notions that we're watching the deft moves of a political chess master. Trump's impulsive bursts are all about dominance. Even when he's being hateful and abusive, calling undocumented Mexican immigrants "animals,"[130] encouraging rally attendees to "knock the crap out of" protesters,[131] and so on, he's assuming the role of conqueror. When Trump yells "He is my type!"[132] in admiration for a politician who body-slams a reporter, the masses cheer. *Sure, Trump's an asshole. But he's our asshole. He defends. He's the top dog. He's a winner!*

Even Trump's famously jarring handshakes are designed to communicate dominance, as he publicly yanks world leaders like France's President Emmanuel Macron and Japan's Prime Minister Shinzo Abe awkwardly onto their toes. Trump pulls a rival into his space and unbalances them. This behavior is no accident. It's a message.

MAGA Republicans are attracted to these kinds of dominance displays, and there are often evolutionary reasons behind this attraction.

---

127 Twitter, August 16, 2017
128 Donald Trump at the United Nations General Assembly, September 19, 2017
129 Fox News Sean Hannity February 28, 2019
130 White House roundtable discussion on California's sanctuary laws May 16, 2018
131 Trump campaign rally February 1, 2016
132 ABC News "Trump: No Regrets for Praising Gianforte for Body-Slamming Reporter" October 19, 2018

The famous Dutch primatologist Frans de Waal has spent decades studying the behavior of dominant primates and their subordinates. In his 1982 book *Chimpanzee Politics*, de Waal observed the structured hierarchies of chimpanzee colonies. In each example the alpha male exerted authority and intimidated subordinates and rivals through threats, intimidation, and overt aggression. The alpha also engaged in a kind of deal-making with other high-status males to consolidate power. When challenged, the alpha chimp screamed and flailed in chaotic protest as rivals and underlings scrambled or cowered in fear. When order was restored, group members reengaged the alpha in various gestures of submission.

Frans de Wall described a specific example of this scenario involving an alpha chimp named Yeroen. The author describes the aftermath of a challenge and Yeroen's explosive response:

> As suddenly as the din had begun, peace would return. Yeroen would seat himself, and the other apes would hasten to pay their respects to him. Like a king he accepted this mass homage as his due, obviously regarding some of his subjects as unworthy even of a glance.[133]

As many White House staffers can attest, this scenario is genuinely Trumpian. The 2020 book *A Very Stable Genius: Donald J. Trump's Testing of America* reveals example after example of Donald Trump's "rages and frenzies" when challenged. His tirades are unhinged, paranoid, and cruel. He is the alpha. He is not to be contested. As Trump told *People* magazine back in 1981, "Man is the most vicious of all animals, and life is a series of battles ending in victory or defeat."[134] In Trump's world, cooperation and compromise are expressions of weakness. To the victor go the spoils.

There's a great deal of science regarding our evolutionary psychology. Every day, people are lauded or dismissed because of their stature,

---

133 Chapter Two Chimpanzee Politics: Power and Sex Among Apes Frans de Waal 1982
134 The Strange Case of Donald J. Trump: A Psychological Reckoning Dan P. McAdams 2020

their physical strength or athletic prowess, their influence, their connections, their bank accounts, their conquests, or their status. It's true that complex social interactions don't fit into a cookie cutter, and no doubt human beings have often overridden their genetic programming, but there's no denying the common attraction of the weak toward the strong. Strength is power. Power is dominance. Dominance is rule. And America rules! Indeed, Trump boasts that the universe itself bows at America's feet.

Donald J. Trump ✔
@realDonaldTrump

Heading to Davos, Switzerland, to meet with World and Business Leaders and bring Good Policy and additional Hundreds of Billions of Dollars back to the United States of America! We are now NUMBER ONE in the Universe, by FAR!!

6:59 PM · Jan 20, 2020 · Twitter for iPhone

As many American evangelicals reject the scientific fact of evolution, they'll likely resist any association of humans with other primates. Such thinking further insulates them from self-examination.

A drive for excellence is a good, necessary, healthy thing, and in many situations, placing that ambition in the framework of contest has merit. Perhaps the best example in recent history is the moon race of the 1960s, where the United States pushed innovation to the limits against the Soviet space program. Sure, Russia's Yuri Gagarin was the first cosmonaut to enter outer space, but Neil Armstrong walked on the moon. In this context the American and Soviet knives sharpened each other and fueled historical achievement.

People have long loved contests with a sole winner or team, and again, the competition galvanizes the effort. The idea that someone must outrun, outrace, outthrow, outswim, outjump, outthink, or out-score a rival crystallizes resolve and focuses the mind and body toward victory. From the soccer pitch to the job interview, life is a game, and opportunity opens its doors to the winners. In this respect, a drive to be number one can be healthy.

But there's something happening in the United States far beyond an estimable appetite for excellence and personal achievement. For many, political opinion seems to reflect a zero-sum game in which winning isn't defined by how fortunate or successful you are but rather by how much taller you stand on the winner's platform, casting a long shadow over those you have vanquished. This opinion doesn't empathize with the losers but instead puffs with ego at their defeat. The Fox News conservative easily boasts to all other nations that, try as they might, they'll never achieve the greatness of the United States. *We're number one.*

Fine. Let's validate this claim. Which metrics reveal our superiority? What do the numbers say?

Average Income: The honors go to Monaco. Gross national income per capita is over $186,000, by far the highest in the world. Liechtenstein and Bermuda are ranked two and three respectively, both averaging six-figure incomes. Switzerland ranks fourth, still more than $84,000, followed by Norway, Macao, Luxembourg, and Iceland.[135]

At $63,080, the United States ranks ninth for average personal income per capita, just a notch above Ireland.

For average income, <u>Monaco</u> is number one.

The Economy: Singapore tops the list. Even allowing for variables like the cost of living, taxes, and so on, there's no arguing that Singapore has surpassed the United States in terms of technological advancement, skilled labor, and business innovation. In fact, in 2019 the IMB

---

135 WorldData.info "Average Income Around the World"

World Competitiveness Center named Singapore the world's most competitive economy, and the World Economic Forum put Singapore at the top of its Global Competitive Index rankings.

Among first-world nations, in terms of median income and economic strength, <u>Singapore</u> is number one.

Largest Army: And the winner is…China. Statista, a German online portal for statistics, released its data on The Largest Armies in the World Based on Active Military Personnel in 2019, and China topped that list with 2,183,000 active military men and women. The United States could do no better than third place at just over half of China's number.[136] India was number two.

The United States easily took the top slot on the question of military *spending*. In 2018 America spent $649 billion dollars, a number that is down from 2012 after the downscaling of war efforts in Iraq and Afghanistan, and seems on track to remain consistent in that zone. Interestingly, it's projected that between 2013 and 2022 the United States will spend more than half of its budget on nuclear weapons,[137] weapons designed not to be used but which instead promise a "mutually assured destruction" that keeps other nations from pressing the nuclear button. The U.S. hasn't detonated a nuke in wartime since Nagasaki.

In terms of a standing army, <u>China</u> is number one.

Peace: Iceland wins this one, followed by New Zealand, Portugal, Austria, Denmark, Canada, Singapore, Slovenia, Japan, the Czech Republic, Switzerland, Ireland, Australia, and Finland. The United States isn't even in the top twenty. The ranking is part of an annual analysis called The Global Peace Index, a list produced by the Institute for Economics and Peace. It meshes key indicators such as involvement in military conflict, statistics for violent crime, incarceration

---

136 Statista "The Largest Armies in the World Based on Active Military Personnel in 2019"
137 Statista "The 15 Countries with the Highest Military Spending Worldwide in 2018"

---

rates, risk of natural disaster, life satisfaction surveys, and so on.

In terms of peacefulness, <u>Iceland</u> is number one.

Quality of Life: In 2018 *U.S. News and World Report* teamed up with BAV Group and The Wharton School of the University of Pennsylvania to analyze the variables that constitute a good or poor quality of life. Those variables included affordability, the job market, innovation, political stability, economic stability, income equality, family-friendliness, public education, public safety, and healthcare.

In terms of quality of life, <u>Canada</u> is number one.

Education: 2015 PISA data published by the Pew Research Center has Singapore ranking highest globally in science, mathematics, and reading.[138] Japan ranked second, Estonia third, and then Taiwan, Finland, Macao, Canada, Vietnam, Hong Kong, and South Korea.

The United States ranks thirty-eighth out of seventy-one countries in math and twenty-fourth in science and reading literacy.

In terms of education, <u>Singapore</u> is number one.

Healthcare: A 2017 analysis of overall health metrics (methods of care, ease of access, efficiency, distribution, and outcomes) ranks the United Kingdom, Australia, and the Netherlands first, second, and third, respectively.[139] Despite spending far more than other high-income countries on healthcare—more than 16 percent of its Gross Domestic Product[140]—the United States doesn't clear the top ten.

In terms of healthcare, the <u>United Kingdom</u> is number one.

Life Expectancy: CIA's *The World Factbook* averaged the lifespans of people born in the same year. Averaging 89.40 years is the nation

---

138 Pew Research Center "2015 Program for International Student Assessment"
139 The Commonwealth Fund study 2017
140 OECD Health Data 2016 "Health Care Spending as a Percentage of GDP, 1980–2014"

of Monaco. Japan sees average lifespans of 85, followed closely by Singapore, Macau, San Marino, Iceland, and Hong Kong. The United States ranks forty-third with an average lifespan of eighty.[141]

In terms of life expectancy, <u>Monaco</u> is number one.

Cultural Influence: Italy is the country that is most fashionable, trendy, modern, and culturally significant.[142] For its cuisine, clothing, furniture, art, entertainment, and so on, the *U.S. News and World Report*'s "2020 Best Countries Report" ranked Italy as the strongest in overall cultural identity, followed by France and Spain. Despite its $717 billion media and entertainment industry, the United States ranks fourth on the list.

In terms of cultural influence, <u>Italy</u> is number one.

Most Powerful: Finally, the United States wins the prize, consistently dominating news headlines, engaging policymakers, exerting military influence, and shaping world economic patterns. The U.S. leads the so-called war on terror, is NATO's largest contributor, has the biggest military budget, and boasts the world's largest overall economy. Russia and China rank number two and number three respectively.

In terms of power, the <u>United States</u> is number one.

Best Overall: Combining the above factors into a larger whole, out of seventy-tree ranked nations, Best in Show goes to Switzerland, one of the planet's wealthiest countries.[143] Canada came in second. Japan third. Germany and Australia rounded out the top five. The United States ranked seventh.

In terms of being the Greatest Country in the World, <u>Switzerland</u> is number one.

Perhaps most interestingly, according to the 2016 YouGov International

---

141 CIA.gov The World Factbook "Country Comparison Life Expectancy at Birth" 2019
142 U.S. News and World Report "2020 Best Countries Report"
143 U.S. News and World Report "2020 Best Countries Report"

Survey on Globalization, the U.S. ranks first in **National Pride**, with 41 percent of citizens firmly convinced that it is the best country in the world. Yet Americans are distrustful and often dissatisfied about the inner workings of their own nation. Four out of ten admit they "strongly dislike" their president. Seventy percent distrust the "crooked" politicians in office. Sixty-four percent say that the United States is "divided between ordinary people and the corrupt elites who exploit them."[144] The messages clash against each other. We're the greatest—and we're poorly led, corrupt, and divided.

It's true that the United States is experiencing profound discontent. So why are so many conservatives defiantly planting American victory flags? Looking back to my own former attitudes, I suspect two major reasons: *insecurity* and *ignorance*.

The privileged perch on a fragile rung of the ladder, a few steps beyond a "different" America. They fear a diversity of people and ideas, so they overcompensate with anthems about the greatness of our past and the need to resurrect it. Hence President Trump's conservative war cry: "Make America Great Again."

In my devout Republican days, I also fretted about the potential death of America's cultural identity. In the early 1990s, 40 percent of Americans identified as politically conservative, but liberals were increasing in number and influence, infecting America's red, white, and blue with unseemly shades of gray. Those repugnant Democrats clutched a utopian hash-pipe dream about a borderless planet, the kumbaya fantasy of tree-hugging Berkeley types still buzzing from Woodstock. Liberals were of a different stripe, a different mind, and a different set of values. They oozed permissiveness and spurned the traditional family. They disrespected our veterans with war protests. They aborted their own children without conscience. They sought the legalization of harmful drugs. They were soft on crime. And they admired (gasp!) other cultures. Had they no structure, boundaries, or

---

144 YouGov Cambridge Globalism Project, in tandem with Cambridge University and The Guardian May 2019

limits? What kind of anarchistic America did they wish to inflict upon the rest of us?

Conservativism had plenty of structure, which made me feel safe. There was little motivation to peek over the fence, evolve an idea, or expand my horizon, and my notions about America's distant past were whitewashed bumper stickers. Columbus discovered the new world (in truth, he stumbled upon the Americas by accident). The Founding Fathers were devout Christians (many weren't) who were champions of freedom (some were slave owners). George Washington could not tell a lie (biographer Mason Locke Weems invented the famous cherry tree myth in 1800). The Constitution promoted my religion (it doesn't contain a single mention of God).

Closer to home, my conceptions of "the good old days"—1950s America—was a romanticized Beaver Cleaver postcard depicting the nuclear family, after-church socials, teen chastity, Bill Haley on the jukebox, white-collar affluence, and a *literal* black-and-white cultural attitude on big issues. Today I chuckle at my own naive imaginings about the era (think *Mad Men* produced by Pat Robertson), and I've gotten a better look at the realities behind the airbrushing.

It's true that the 1950s enjoyed post-war economic success and relative global peace, but domestically, that decade was a mess, its Ozzie-and-Harriet veneer masking a cauldron of cultural discontent, racial discrimination, anti-gay bigotry, sexual repression, and fear.

In 1950, women had enjoyed the Constitutional right to vote for only thirty years, and their assigned roles often required subservience to men under a biblical model: "Wives, submit to your own husbands, as to the LORD. For the husband is the head of the wife even as Christ is the head of the church, his body, and is himself its Savior. Now as the church submits to Christ, so also wives should submit in everything to their husbands" (Ephesians 5:22-24). Even women who attended college were ostensibly there to get an "M.R.S. degree"—a husband. Women not married by the age of thirty were usually deemed old maids and damaged goods. American propaganda contrasted the ostensibly horrible lives of Russian women, depicted in gunnysacks, working in dismal factories, against the bouffant-haired, homebody perfection of the "free" Western wife.[145] The good American woman was expected to appreciate her role as homemaker, polishing up like a porcelain doll for *her man*, darning his socks, and having dinner on the table by five thirty. These stereotypes were constantly reinforced by American television programs such as *The Donna Reed Show*.

Illustration: "Stainless Bliss" by Vintagraph

Wives were encouraged to bear children soon after wedlock,[146] and American Christianity frequently encouraged large families ("Be

---

145 PBS American Experience "Mrs. America: Women's Roles in the 1950s"
146 "Estimated Median Age at First Marriage, by Sex: 1890 to Present" U.S. Bureau of the Census

fruitful and multiply." Genesis 1:28). Unwed mothers were shunned by society, and pregnant teenagers were often forced to drop out of school and shipped away to maternity "homes for wayward girls" far from the disapproving eyes of polite society. The babies were often ripped from their teen moms in forced adoptions.[147]

The United States had self-fitted its own chastity belt, with parents and preachers admonishing the *Rebel Without A Cause* youth culture for its leather pants and sinful rock and roll. When Elvis Presley sang "Hound Dog" on the Ed Sullivan Show September 9, 1956, TV camera operators were ordered to frame him only from the waist up, because gyrating hips were considered suggestive and sexual.

Racial segregation was common across the United States. Black schools and white schools. Water fountains designated for whites and blacks. Separation on public buses—blacks in the back. Separate sections for restaurant dining, with separate entry doors based on race. Separate sections in movie theaters, usually relegating blacks to the balcony. Even public swimming pools were segregated, because so many white Americans feared the filth and disease supposedly carried by African Americans.[148] The few unsegregated pools posted separate swimming hours for whites and blacks, with thorough chlorination and scrubbing scheduled in the interim.

After the historic 1954 Supreme Court ruling Brown v. Board of Education mandated the national desegregation of public schools, white supremacists organized massive resistance. In March 1956, 101 U.S. congressmen signed the Declaration of Constitutional Principles, known as the Southern Manifesto, opposing public race integration. Black students attempting to integrate into formerly white schools faced angry mobs and violent threats, requiring many to be escorted into school buildings by members of the National Guard. In September 1958, Arkansas Governor Orval Faubus closed all Little Rock high schools for the entire year to prevent African American

---

147 The Girls Who Went Away: The Hidden History of Women Who Surrendered Children for Adoption in the Decades Before Roe v. Wade by Ann Fessler 2007
148 NPR "Racial History of American Swimming Pools" The Bryant Park Project May 6, 2008

students from attending, his order affirmed by a public vote with 70 percent approval.[149] After the dissolution of black schools, black teachers faced massive job losses as white America favored white candidates. Communities remained largely segregated, and black families navigated onerous poverty and societal blacklisting.

The LGBT Americans of the 1950s were largely shunned and often threatened physically. The few gay advocacy groups faced massive resistance. The American Psychiatric Association Diagnosis and Statistical Manual (DSM) still listed homosexuality as an illness, a designation not changed until 1973.[150] Gays were forbidden to serve in the military, as President Harry S. Truman had signed the May 6, 1950, Uniform Code of Military Justice, which forbade "unnatural carnal copulation with another person of the same or opposite sex or with an animal." President Eisenhower followed up with the April 27, 1953, Executive Order 10450, which legally justified investigating and firing gay employees. Soldiers discovered to be gay were discharged. Same-sex adoption was illegal. Gay marriage was illegal. Even gay reading material was challenged as obscene, with *ONE: The Homosexual Magazine* sued in the Supreme Court for violations of obscenity laws.[151]

It was a paranoid decade. The year 1953 saw America executing its own citizens for spying. Julius and Ethel Rosenberg were convicted of passing nuclear secrets to the Soviets, and both were killed in the electric chair on June 19 of that year. Public fears about communist Russian spies ran rampant, as demonstrated by Joseph McCarthy's demagogic Senate subcommittee hearings against American government officials, Hollywood celebrities, media moguls such as Edward R. Murrow, and even soldiers in the United States Army.

After the Soviet Union detonated its first nuclear device on August 29, 1949, the United States scrambled in Cold War panic about the

149 History.com "Little Rock Nine" January 29, 2010
150 U.S. National Library of Medicine, National Institutes of Health "Out of DSM: Depathologizing Homosexuality," Jack Drescher December 4, 2015
151 U.S. Supreme Court, One, Inc. v. Olesen 1958. Ruled in the magazine's favor.

atomic bomb, subjecting frightened schoolchildren to bomb-related safety films and "duck and cover" drills in case of nuclear attack. (I'm still unsure how hiding under a table protects someone from a thermonuclear blast.)

Image: a 1952 Civil Defense comic book preparing children for nuclear attack

Another Soviet development—the launch of *Sputnik 1* on October 4, 1957—prompted terrors about an enemy nuclear launch from space. Scientists who originally developed the WW2 nukes, aghast at what they had created, founded the organization Bulletin of the Atomic Scientists, which portended impending annihilation with a symbolic Doomsday Clock. Mid-twentieth century America feared the End of the World.

In my Fox News conservatism, I was blind to the dark shades of "the good old days." I also waved the banner of national superiority because it fit my religious worldview, an opinion of America long ago branded onto my brain by authority: my parents, my pastors, my Christian schoolteachers. Ages before Donald Trump's America First campaign, Republicans deified their nation with hyperbole—greatest, most, best—and laid claim to the divine favor of Christ. As the famous anthem declares,

> *Our father's God! to thee,*
> *Author of Liberty, to thee we sing;*
> *Soon may our land be bright,*
> *With holy freedom's right,*
> *Protect us by thy might, Great God, our King.*[152]

In an uglier framework, factions of American conservatism wax nostalgic for times of demographic dominance and political power. Even among many Republicans who correctly repudiate racist hate groups such as the Aryan Brotherhood and the Ku Klux Klan, there remains a yearning for simpler times when the sandbox was small, the genders played their roles, the colors didn't blend, and Christian nationalism ruled. When faced with today's cultural evolutions and the rise of progressivism, many conservatives lock their doors and retreat to their corners. The future is coming. And it frightens them. Hence the overcompensation born of insecurity, rooted in ignorance, fueled by the fear of change, and convinced that shouting "We're number one" makes the claim true by mere declaration. (Again, the U.S. is ranked number one in national pride.)

Yet if I may be so ironic as to quote from Proverbs, "pride goes before destruction." Pride distorts perception. It is so often divisive... the ugly exhibition of a superiority complex that perceives others as inferior and disqualified. Is this how a nation wishes to buttress its self-esteem? Wouldn't a healthier attitude commit itself to earning achievement instead of forging its transcripts? Shouldn't a noble nation acknowledge the true winners while continuing to better itself?

Beyond that, wouldn't a more globalist mindset be better for everyone, including the United States? I'm not saying I'm opposed to national borders, nor am I callow enough to think that 195 global countries would ever hold hands in harmony, but now more than

---

152 "America (My Country, 'Tis of Thee), Samuel Francis Smith 1831

ever, a connected world offers us the opportunity to forge alliances in good faith, to join with other nations sharing worthy values, and to use those partnerships to defeat the destructive forces that infect the human condition. We can remember that the boundaries that divide us were once drawn by subjective, human hands, and that those boundaries sometimes need to be moved or abolished outright. Good fences don't always make good neighbors; sometimes they foster xenophobia, ignorance, fear, and hatred.

To many, especially in the Trump era, borders and walls are proud American symbols. They represent strength and superiority, and they provide a perception of safety. Often these borders are necessary, but they should not be the defining symbol of a nation—populated by immigrants—that prides itself on liberty, and I remain convinced that a greater outward focus would help lift the tide that raises all ships.

Cooperation is good for others, which in turn is good for us. Association conquers alienation. Friendship conquers prejudice. Humility conquers hubris. We can pursue truth beyond mere claims. We can be honest about our mistakes and flaws with a commitment to improve. We can spurn injustice on both sides of a national line. We can approach with charity and enthusiasm those who are different from us. And we can celebrate the beautiful human spectrum of color and culture with every intention of embracing its best attributes. We can address the genuine dangers of this world without lumping huge groups into guilt by association. We can assess and challenge the world's superstitions while advocating for those who still practice them. We can observe the world, not merely in terms of competing nations but as beings who—down to our genetic core—are of the same family. Across the planet, our DNA is 99.9 percent identical. We are all the human condition.[153]

Imagine if we put down our nationalistic banners to look across borders, oceans, races, colors, and cultures and start to see ourselves.

What a world that would be!

---

153 National Human Genome Research Institute "Genetics and Genomics Fact Sheet"

CHAPTER SIX:

This Means War: Manufactured Persecution in Defense of Christian Privilege

IT WAS THE fall of 2015, and war had been declared. A war on Christmas.

The American coffee company Starbucks had just released its seasonal beverage cups, and they were red. Holiday red. The design no longer bore snowflakes (2013), snowmen (2012), art deco ice skaters (2011), inspirational messages (2010), or ornaments (2008–2009). Continuing a two-decade tradition of specialized cups, the new offering featured simple red with some wintery-design shading. Starbucks vice president Jeffrey Fields had announced that the company "wanted to usher in the holidays with a purity of design that welcomes all of our stories."[154]

Evangelical social media personality Joshua Feuerstein was having none of this. He saw the Starbucks heresy as an attempt to erase Jesus Christ from Christ's own holiday and yet another secular salvo against a Christian nation, so he posted a Facebook protest video with this accusation:

---

154 Starbucks press release, October 22, 2015

 **Joshua Feuerstein**
November 5, 2015 · 🌐   •••

Starbucks REMOVED CHRISTMAS from their cups because they hate Jesus ... SO I PRANKED THEM ... and they HATE IT!!!! #share
Use #MERRYCHRISTMASSTARBUCKS
Follow --> **Joshua Feuerstein**

In the video Feuerstein frothed about the "political correctness" that had caused a corporate powerhouse to strike his personal savior from their brand. (Note that Christ hadn't appeared on cups in years past.) In Josh's mind, Starbucks hadn't chosen the red design for reasons of aesthetics or the marketplace. It had done so "because they hate Jesus." The apparent Starbucks policy of having its employees wish customers "Happy holidays" instead of "Merry Christmas" was salt in that freshly opened wound. Feuerstein's video urged viewers to offer "Merry Christmas" as their customer names to be called out when their coffees were ready. Christians would force their savior back into the public milieu.

This clip went viral with more than ten million views. It was everywhere. Feuerstein's tempest in a coffee cup even landed him on major news outlets such as CNN, where Josh boasted, "I think Starbucks has gotten the message that the Christian majority in this country has awakened and are demanding that our voice be heard."[155]

Starbucks likely basked in the free publicity, which it has enjoyed every Christmas since. In fact, the Google search phrase "Starbucks holiday cup controversy" has auto-fill options for every year since 2015. A Starbucks online promotional video introducing the 2017 holiday cup included two women holding hands, which prompted a *BuzzFeed* article titled "People Are Saying Starbucks' New Holiday

---

155 CNN "Starbucks' Plain Red Holiday Cups Stir Up Controversy" November 9, 2015

Cup is Totally Gay."[156] The cups themselves featured a festive print with the androgynous locked hands of two unseen characters. Twitter exploded around a single word: *Lesbians!* Shrewdly, Starbucks refused to confirm or deny. The public inference about gay love prompted indignant posts with Bible verses like Romans 1:26: "Because of this, God gave them over to shameful lusts. Even their women exchanged natural sexual relations for unnatural ones." The dust-up was featured in posts by *The New York Times*, the conservative media company *The Blaze*, and of course, Fox News.

In 2019 Starbucks heaped burning coals upon the heads of Christian fundamentalists with its sacrilegious holiday cups bearing the words, "Merry Coffee" and impassioned keyboard warriors rewarded them again with months of free advertising.

To be fair, I must admit that most of the Starbucks outrage existed in religious fringes and on news outlets eager for controversy and clicks. My Christian friends and family didn't believe that Starbucks was attacking Jesus Christ, but family members did—and still do—believe that secular activists were waging a war on Christmas. On the 2016 campaign trail, President Donald Trump often tapped into that nerve with declarations that America's federally protected holiday was being threatened by a liberal gag order, telling a cheering crowd in Manchester, New Hampshire, that "You are going to be able to say 'Merry Christmas' again!"[157] Yes, previously oppressed Americans forced to vomit out generic holiday greetings had been liberated at the vocal chords, their champion controlling the spoken language of more than 300 million citizens and—literally—saving the savior.

This was followed by Eric Trump's false 2016 claim that former President Barack Obama had sacrilegiously renamed the White House National Christmas Tree a "holiday tree,"[158] and that Obama

---

156 Buzzfeed "People Are Saying Starbucks' New Holiday Cup is Totally Gay" November 15, 2017
157 Trump campaign rally, SNHU Arena, February 2016
158 BuzzFeed "Eric Trump: My Dad Ran Because the White House Christmas Tree is Now a 'Holiday Tree'" August 26, 2016

had whitewashed Christ out of his own birthday. Note Obama's easily searchable Twitter history of overtly saying "Christmas" and "Merry Christmas" since 2009.

Barack Obama ✓
@BarackObama

Michelle receives this year's White House Christmas tree yesterday. Watch the video: http://bit.ly/4o90RN

6:13 PM · Nov 28, 2009 · Twitter Web Client

Granted, the name Trump is rarely synchronized with the word "truth," but Trump's bloviations played well to a Christian audience primed to feel persecuted—primed by their churches, their pastors, their privilege, and their chosen news authority, Fox News.

Before his ignominious exit from Fox News prime time in 2017 over allegations of sexual harassment, Bill O'Reilly was one of the most powerful broadcast voices in America. He'd risen through the ranks in local news and tabloid television to helm Fox's *The O'Reilly Factor* in 1996, which dominated cable news for sixty consecutive ratings quarters.[159] O'Reilly was a self-described "culture warrior" (a term that was also the title of his 2007 bestselling book) battling the secular progressives who sought to destroy traditional American values.

The road to O'Reilly's success had been paved by the terrorist attacks of September 11, the Second Iraq War, and a Republican White House helmed by a president—George W. Bush—who had also been on a "crusade" against America's enemies.[160] Especially from the Fox News vantage, it seemed that the United States was under assault from without and within. But while President Bush was selling his war against terrorism over Saddam Hussein's (nonexistent) weapons of mass destruction, Bill O'Reilly was selling his own pet scare about

---

159 MEDIAite "Q1 2015 Ratings: CNN Makes Big Demo Gaines, MSNBC Hits Record Lows, Fox Continues Victories" March 31, 2015
160 The White House "Remarks by the President Upon Arrival" September 16, 2001

---

the culture war at home: the war on Christmas.

On December 24, 2004, O'Reilly opened his "Talking Points Memo" with the words "Christmas under siege" and lamented the anti-American encroachment of secular progressives who "realize that America as it is now will never approve of gay marriage, partial birth abortion, euthanasia, legalized drugs, income redistribution through taxation, and many other progressive visions."[161] His statement echoed the evangelical party line, that the United States requires Judeo-Christian philosophy to "defeat terrorism and any other evil." So when the popular retailer Macy's favored employee greetings of "Happy holidays" over "Merry Christmas" in its stores, that directive wasn't seen as a gesture of inclusion. It was a move toward "terrorism and any other evil." It was a crack in the shield protecting righteous America from the slippery slope of moral chaos.

Despite our own Supreme Court's ultimate affirmation of the legitimacy of same-sex marriage, Bill O'Reilly didn't see marriage equality as an American value (or apparently a human right) but as a betrayal of the national religion, specifically his own. Notice how he also set his Judeo-Christian standard against the issues of a woman's bodily autonomy, the right to death with dignity, the legality of recreational drugs, and new taxpayer-funded social programs. From his (Catholic) vantage, these weren't ideas to be discussed and addressed on their merits by a free and democratic society. They were supernaturally settled law. As such, O'Reilly—culture warrior—promised his audience that he would "use all the power that I have on radio and television to bring horror into the world of people" who "diminish and denigrate the [Christmas] holiday."[162]

The message was clear: *Today the progressives come for Christmas. Tomorrow they'll come for Christ.*

Even if this persecution narrative was true, I'm unsure why an

---

161 Fox News, The O'Reilly Factor December 24, 2004
162 Fox News, The Radio Factor with Bill O'Reilly, December 2, 2005

omnipotent Christ would be at all worried about the maneuverings of puny human liberals. Certainly the Almighty could smite any lefty heathens who dared to slight him on his birthday. The Reverend Dr. Paul Baxley, executive coordinator of the Cooperative Baptist Fellowship, agreed, stating, "To suggest that the church needs the protection of the state in order to flourish and thrive is idolatrous."[163] Yet the evangelicals continued their panic.

Fox News remains one of the biggest megaphones for the war on Christmas, often to great comedic effect. A few recent examples include the following:

- Tucker Carlson recently frothed with outrage over a baker at the Scottish Parliament café who prepared holiday gingerbread people instead of gingerbread men. The on-screen chyron read "Political Correctness Targets Cookies" as Carlson bemoaned this "spiritual neutering" and told his audience that "the war on Christmas is a global struggle."[164]

- Sean Hannity wailed about a Massachusetts church that put its nativity Jesus doll in a cage to protest President Trump's border separation policy. After posting a now-deleted tweet saying "CHRISTMAS IS UNDER SEIGE,[165] Hannity introduced video of the caged doll with the words "You probably don't want your kids to watch this.[166] On that same day, Fox News's Laura Ingraham continued the cage outrage as her guest, right wing radio host Dan Bongino, called liberals a "blowtorch on everything."[167] Strange that these hosts seemed unperturbed about the caging of actual human beings.

- On *Fox & Friends*, conservative talk show host Dennis Prager said that "kids no longer have Christmas vacation—holiday

---

163 ChristiansAgainstChristianNationalism.org
164 Fox News, Tucker Carlson Tonight, December 18, 2018
165 Newsweek "Sean Hannity Says 'Christmas is under Siege' as Twitter Users Have a Field Day at his Expense" December 6, 2018
166 Fox News, Sean Hannity, December 5, 2018
167 Fox News, The Ingraham Angle, December 5, 2018

vacation! Companies no longer have Christmas parties—holiday parties! And of course, it's 'Happy Holidays,' not 'Merry Christmas.'" His argument wasn't that Christmas vacations, parties, and greetings had been ripped from the public domain, but that "radicals" had the gall to voluntarily refer to the occasion in broader terms.[168] (Those inclusive bastards!)

This righteous indignation is made even more ludicrous when one realizes that most American Christmas traditions are rooted in ancient paganism. The Christmas tree and Christmas gifts came from the festival of Saturnalia. December 25 marked the winter solstice celebrations in anticipation of longer days and the coming harvests. Mistletoe was considered a magical fertility plant by first-century Druids. Yuletide was a Germanic party involving ghosts. The modern depictions of Santa Claus reflect the white-bearded Norse god Odin. Even those Christians spontaneously combusting over the Christ-canceling abbreviation "Xmas" can't be bothered to do a quick Google search. The X represents the Greek letter chi, the first letter in the Greek word for Christ, *Χριστός*.

So much smoke. So little fire.

I remember when Fox News carried the 2011 Associated Press story about my hometown, Tulsa, dropping the word *Christmas* from its annual Parade of Lights, and even Oklahoma Senator Jim Inhofe refused to participate because "If Jesus isn't there, I'm not there."[169] Inhofe—like the indignant Tulsans who organized an alternative Christmas parade—felt that his god had been insulted, and he took personal offense. Yet the Parade of Lights name change had been informed by an attitude of inclusion, perhaps best summed up by a Tulsa mother quoted in an AP report: "As the world gets smaller and we come in contact with other people who are not like ourselves or practice other religions, it seems to be a no-brainer to open your arms to celebrate with them because they're your neighbors." The Parade of Lights

---

168 Fox & Friends, December 16, 2019
169 Fox News, "With No 'Christmas,' Tulsa Group Plans Own Parade" December 8, 2011

wasn't locking Christians out. It was inviting others in.

Christian nationalists shudder at notions about inclusion. Inclusion means sharing the table, making room for others, dissolving the monopoly. Sure, the November–January months have many other holidays representing many other faiths, including Islamic, Jewish, Buddhist, Wiccan, Pagan, and more, but those faiths are stowaways on the Good Ship Christianity, robbing precious resources from legitimate passengers. Provision for others means stealing from the One. (This attitude also permeates many Republican attitudes about immigrants, but that's a topic for another day.)

In my religious years, this persecution narrative permeated my thinking. I remember guest-hosting the morning show on the conservative talk station 1170 AM KFAQ in 2005, then a Fox News affiliate, frothing at my broadcast microphone about the annual assault on Jesus's birthday. I sounded much like Fox News host John Gibson, who had just released his book, *The War on Christmas: How the Liberal Plot to Ban the Sacred Christian Holiday is Worse than You Thought*. I was indignant about those secular schemers coming after my holiday, my God, my country, so I pounded the drums of brave resistance.

Of course, my freedom of religion remained in full effect as I wailed about the liberal attack on my religious liberties. I could give Christmas gifts. I could organize Christmas events. I could fill my yard with religiously themed Christmas decorations. I could attend Christmas pageants at Christian churches at any hour of any day. I could decorate my Christmas tree and hang Christmas lights. I could join a caroling troupe and sing Christmas songs door to door without reprisal. I could watch Christmas television specials (*A Charlie Brown Christmas* remains a favorite) and cue Mariah Carey's "All I Want for Christmas is You" on the CD player. And I could freely wish anyone, anywhere, a merry Christmas without a care.

For a guy whose religious freedom was under attack, I enjoyed an awful lot of latitude, and this remains true for all American Christians well beyond the holidays. They can freely speak Christian words, attend Christian worship services, enroll in Christian schools, evangelize Christian doctrine, say Christian prayers, enjoy Christian radio stations, watch Christian television, read Christian books, shop at Christian retailers, wear Christian apparel, get Christian tattoos, erect Christian billboards, display Christian messages, and openly reflect Christianity into their circles of influence for three hundred sixty-five days every year. Their churches enjoy tax-exempt status. They enjoy strategically placed Bibles in the rooms of major hotel chains (ever seen a Qur'an in there, folks?). The majority of their elected officials have some connection to the Christian religion.[170] Their lives represent pure Constitutional liberty and strong protections for a private and personal faith. Yet many still cry "persecution!" Why is this? I think the answer is twofold.

First, Christ himself declared that good Christians must endure oppression for his sake: "Yea, and all that will live godly in Christ Jesus shall suffer persecution"—2 Timothy 3:12. The thinking goes like this: if you're not under attack from Satan, you must be of no concern to the devil, which means you're spiritually impotent. A good Christian is a genuine threat to Satan and always under siege. So how does a spoiled-rotten American Christian enjoying constitutional protection achieve persecution to obtain glory? Simple. He manufactures the persecution.

Christianity is imbued with military language. I can sing from memory the children's hymn taught to me at Vacation Bible School, a song that first injected the "war on Christianity" narrative into my young brain:

I may never march in the infantry
Ride in the cavalry
Shoot the artillery
I may never shoot for the enemy,
But I'm in the Lord's army.

---

170 Pew Forum "Faith on the Hill: The Religious Composition of the 116th Congress" January 3, 2019

Interestingly, we marched as we sang, fists closed and arms swinging like we were in a military parade.

The Lord's Army had long sounded the trumpet with classic hymns like "The Battle Belongs to the Lord," "Put on the Armor of God," and "Onward, Christian Soldiers." These anthems spoke of marches and banners and armies and triumph. "Forward into battle" was the rallying cry.

Contemporary Christian Music (CCM), the soundtrack of my youth, featured plenty of military imagery. Christian metal band Stryper released the 1985 album *Soldiers Under Command*, with the band posing as machine-gunners on the cover. Petra's 1987 album *This Means War* featured song titles such as, "Get on Your Knees and Fight Like a Man." Carman's 1993 single "God's Got an Army" was an overt Christian nationalist anthem, with the lyrics proclaiming that "There's joy in the battle, so we commence to change this nation's course." Morgan Cryar's 1986 hit song "Pray in the USA"[171] was especially sobering, as it warned of a future totalitarian government stripping American Christians of their rights:

> Someday we may hear it
> "Prayin' is a felony"
> I guess they'll call us criminals then
> I guess that's what I'll be.

Cryar's audiences gobbled up this anthem like candy, and I gladly joined in. Christian culture was constantly validating my divine claim on America's sacred ground. The more freedom I enjoyed, the more I bemoaned the secular assault on my freedoms. This constantly cultivated in me an attitude of righteous indignation and moral superiority. Notions of persecution had galvanized Christ's recruit, and my resistance to this persecution had made me worthy. I was a Walter Mitty-esque man who indulged his largely homogenous days with fantasies of religious victory. Across the board, this remains a common attitude among American Christians.

---

171 Morgan Cryar, Fuel on the Fire album, Star Song Music

Secondly, the "war on Christianity" narrative has the effect of painting oppressors as victims, a tactic used by the privileged against the underprivileged throughout recorded history. One can almost hear the indignant cries of nineteenth-century plantation owners who invoked the biblical Abraham in the defense of owning slaves, their Bibles used as conversation stoppers, God's ruling beyond question. Inequality of the races was a matter of divine design, and any shift away from God's blueprint risked disaster. As the confederacy's Alexander Stephens famously said, "It is not for us to inquire into the wisdom of His ordinances, or to question them."[172] Stephens and the confederacy argued that the liberation of black people inflicted burden upon white people economically, socially, and religiously.

Five years before the passing of the Nineteenth Amendment, U.S. Congressmen denied voting rights to women, claiming that the suffragists would sabotage God's design. As Florida Democrat Frank Clark said on the House floor in 1915 that "any attempt to change this order of human affairs is an attempt to change and to overthrow one of the solemn decrees of God Almighty."[173]

These men weren't being asked to sacrifice liberties of their own but merely to afford those same liberties to others. Over this they sounded the alarms of oppression. Majority classes have long done the same. They enjoy their power and influence. They dislike sharing the table. And so it is with American Christians watching their majority ebb against the rising wave of non-Christians.

In 2019, the Pew Research Center released an analysis of the religious landscape of the United States, and the numbers were telling. When asked about their religion, 65 percent of respondents described themselves as Christian, a decline of 12 percent in ten years. Protestantism and Catholicism also saw significant losses, and today those denominations represent only 43 percent of the U.S. population.

---

172 Alexander H. Stephens "Corner Stone" speech, March 21, 1861
173 U.S. House of Representatives, January 12, 1915

After Christianity, Judaism is the second largest religious affiliation in the United States, yet 20 percent of American Jews describe themselves as having no religion.[174] Their Judaism is cultural, not supernatural. In fact, Robert Putnam and David Campbell's 2012 book *American Grace: How Religion Divides and Unites Us* documents that half of all American Jews actually have doubts about the existence of God, and a huge swath of observant Jews support a humanist philosophy over a supernatural belief.

Muslims currently make up only 1.1 percent of the U.S. population, but their numbers are swelling. The Pew Research Center projects that Muslims will replace Jews as the nation's second-largest religious group by the year 2040.[175]

Meanwhile, people who "describe their religious identity as atheist, agnostic, or 'nothing in particular' (the nones) now stand at 26 percent, up from 17 percent in 2009."[176] A quarter of Americans are effectively non-religious.

Jews. Muslims. Nones. The United States of tomorrow will be more racially, culturally, and religiously diverse. Its people will represent all faiths and none. America's elected officials will look like them, think like them, vote like them. A much wider spectrum of opinions and values will be reflected in the marketplace, the churches, the schools, the courts, the culture. These are not realities to be feared, unless you're a ruling class facing the dissolution of your own monopoly. For the Christian nationalist, informed and potent dissent is terrifying. So sounds the protest cry "Religious liberty!" against all dissenting voices.

Resist the Republican push to institute public-school-sponsored prayers? Challenge the constitutionality of Donald Trump's promise to

---

174 Pew Research Center "A Portrait of Jewish Americans" October 1, 2013
175 Pew Research Center "New Estimates Show U.S. Muslim Population Continues to Grow" January 3, 2018
176 Pew Research Center "In U.S., Decline of Christianity Continues at Rapid Pace" October 17, 2019

---

empower pastors as politicians by repealing the Johnson Amendment? Question Christian prayer meetings held in the Roosevelt Room of the White House? Express concern about Trump's injection of evangelical activists into the judiciary? Oppose efforts by Project Blitz to mandate "In God We Trust" emblems on public vehicles such as police cars? Reject Education Secretary Betsy DeVos's push for taxpayers to fund religious schools via vouchers? Protest the display of Christianity's Ten Commandments on state capitol property in Arkansas? Disagree with the religious justifications for Alabama's draconian abortion ban? Condemn a proposed Texas law that might deny medical care to LGBT people on religious grounds? Support a return to the original motto for the United States, "E Pluribus Unum?" Declare that non-heterosexuals deserve to marry, or that women deserve bodily autonomy, or that non-Christians and secular American citizens should have fair and equal representation? The response is immediate: *"Religious liberty is under attack!"*

Christian nationalists will even turn on less dogmatic Christians. When *Christianity Today* declared that "Trump Should Be Removed from Office" over his "unsavory dealings and immoral acts,"[177] nearly two hundred evangelical leaders slammed the publication, and Trump—laughably—called *Christianity Today* a "far left" magazine.[178] *Christianity Today* had engaged in criticism. Christian nationalists cried oppression.

Ralph Waldo Emerson once wrote in his journal, "Let me never fall into the vulgar mistake of dreaming that I am persecuted whenever I am contradicted."[179] Emerson strikes at the heart of the matter. American Christians aren't being persecuted. They're being contradicted, disagreed with, even rebuffed publicly by other Americans who do not toe the evangelical line. As the saying goes, "When you're accustomed to privilege, equality feels like oppression."

---

177 Christianity Today "Trump Should Be Removed From Office" Mark Galli, December 19, 2019
178 Twitter @realDonaldTrump December 20, 2019
179 Emerson in His Journals by Ralph Waldo Emerson, Harvard University Press April 1984

Perhaps just as irritating to the fundamentalists is the fact that many religious leaders in the United States support a state/church wall. The organization Christians Against Christian Nationalism features believers from various denominations—protestant and Catholic—who resist this assault on the Constitution. Their site features opinions by people such as famous pastor and sociologist Tony Campolo, founder of the Red-Letter Christian movement, who states that "the true Jesus is neither a Republican or a Democrat." Reverend Dr. John Dorhauer, president of the United Church of Christ, says "We are watching core values of and foundational commitment to our Democracy disappear as one of the least Christ-like presidents we have ever seen has forged alliances with Christian nationalists who want to rewrite our Constitution." Sister Simone Campbell, executive director of the Network Lobby for Catholic Social Justice, protests that "Christian nationalism comes from a place of insecurity and fear." (Preach on, sister!)

These pastors get it. They understand the dangers of theocracy. They're untroubled by the idea of a diverse, representative government. And they find President Donald Trump a disastrous bedfellow for anyone claiming moral superiority and the best teachings of Jesus Christ—honesty, respect, forgiveness, humility, charity, and sacrifice.

Tragically the voices of critics are often drowned out by the blustering of mega-pastors like Dr. Robert Jeffress of First Baptist Dallas, a member of Trump's Evangelical Advisory Board and a frequent Fox News contributor. Jeffress gave his congregation the June 24, 2018, sermon, "America is a Christian Nation," which was an interpretive dance between the raindrops. Dr. Jeffress protested that while Thomas Jefferson opposed the governmental establishment of a specific denomination, Jefferson was actually in favor of a governmental faith. It's no mystery which specific faith Jeffress was referring to. In the televised video of his speech, the on-screen chyron read, "The Myth of the 'Separation of Church and State.'"[180] This sermon prompted the *Baptist News* response by another pastor, Andrew Daugherty of Pine Street Church in

---

180 YouTube, Robert Jeffress Sermons, November 9 2018

Colorado, who rightly said, "We are a nation of Christians (and Jews, Muslims, Hindus, Sikhs, Buddhists and people of no faith at all), but we are not a Christian nation."[181]

In an alternate universe, would Dr. Robert Jeffress have preached his sermon to defend a different faith, for example, "America is an Islamic Nation"? I highly doubt it, because his claim of ownership on the U.S. government isn't rooted in noble notions of religious liberty across the belief spectrum. It's rooted in Christian Dominion Theology (government by Christians for Christians to achieve biblical ends) and a desperation to retain power. Jeffress preaches Christian nationalism because it serves his interests. This is problematic. It's divisive. It's anti-American. And it places a single religious group above other American citizens.

As the late Baptist pastor James Dunn often said, "The trouble with a theocracy is everyone wants to be Theo!"[182]

In a defensive posture, Christian nationalists often dress themselves as heroes in good-versus-evil theater. Pastor Jeffress recently told conservative radio host Todd Starnes that there's a "wave of godlessness that is rising in our country," and "we cannot afford to be like German Christians who, in the rise of the evil reign of Adolf Hitler, just remained neutered."[183] (Yes, Jeffress linked American non-Christians to Hitler.) Starnes, a self-professed "gun-toting, Bible-clinging deplorable," hosted a Fox News Radio interview where he affirmed Pastor Jeffress's claim that Democrats worship "the pagan god of the Old Testament, Moloch, who allowed for child sacrifice."[184] (In a rare show of good sense, Fox canceled Starnes's contract after significant public backlash.)

It's bizarre that Pastor Jeffress, the man who proclaimed that Jews are

---

181 Baptist News, "No, Pastor Jeffress (and others), America is Not a Christian Nation. And Here's Why it Matters." Andrew Daugherty July 9, 2018
182 BJC "Truth with the Bark on It: The Wit and Wisdom of James Dunn"
183 ToddStarnes.com "Jeffress: Never Trump Evangelicals are Spineless Morons" February 13, 2019
184 Fox Nation The Todd Starnes Show September 30, 2019

going to Hell,[185] spoke at the opening ceremony of the new American Embassy in Jerusalem. Why would he, along with San Antonio mega-Baptist John Hagee, accept Trump's invitation to lead non-Christians in prayer? I suspect three reasons:

1) He considers Donald Trump—and his invitation to speak—divinely inspired.

2) He's enjoying Trump's preferential treatment of evangelical Christians.

3) His doctrine holds that Israel is a cornerstone for the fulfillment of biblical prophecy and the arrival of the End Times (Zionism).

All three reasons reflect Christian Dominion Theology. America chooses to support a sovereign Jewish Nation for reasons rooted in the Christian Bible. Secretary of State Mike Pompeo said as much when Christian Broadcasting Network interviewer Chris Mitchell asked, "Could it be that President Trump right now has been sort of raised for such a time as this, just like Queen Esther, to help save the Jewish people from the Iranian menace?" Pompeo responded, "As a Christian, I certainly believe that's possible."[186] Pompeo was speaking politically but reasoning religiously. That's scary.

I'm reminded of a slightly more distant example of Christianity's chokehold on Republican ideas. In the wake of the 9/11 attacks on the United States, conservative pundit Ann Coulter wrote that "we should invade their [Muslim] countries, kill their leaders, and convert them to Christianity."[187] Coulter has no tolerance for tolerance, and she despises American liberals, who she claims are in league with Lucifer, as expressed in the title of her 2011 book *Demonic: How the Liberal Mob is Endangering America*. Ann Coulter thinks that liberal values are Satanic values, that "Muslim" equals terrorism, and that

---

185 Trinity Broadcasting Network 2010
186 CBN "Exclusive: Why Secretary of State Mike Pompeo Says Trump is a Possible Queen Esther, Poised to Defend Israel" March 21, 2019
187 Ann Coulter "This is War" National Review September 13, 2001

America has a moral responsibility to spread Christianity, even if it means using the military. These tragic attitudes once infected my own thinking, and they continue to permeate the Christian Right.

As for Trump, he seems quite pleased to be "the chosen one" (his words),[188] and his zealous defenders constantly fuel that fire. Note the religious language:

- "I think that He [God] wanted Donald Trump to become president."[189]—White House Press Secretary Sarah Huckabee Sanders

- "Only God could deliver such a savior to our nation."[190]— Trump campaign manager Brad Parscale

- "Pontius Pilate afforded more rights to Jesus than the Democrats have afforded the President in this [impeachment] process."[191] —Georgia Republican Representative Barry Loudermilk

- "To say no to President Trump would be saying no to God."[192]— Trump spiritual advisor Paula White

- "In the Bible, rain is a sign of God's blessing. And it started to rain, Mr. President, when you came to the platform."[193] — Reverend Franklin Graham

Yes, even the weather affirms God's will! (Or it often rains in Washington, DC.) Graham has long and happily hopped the state-church line, but he slips around the Johnson Amendment by telling people to "vote biblically."[194] It's impossible to miss the Christian nationalism in this instruction, as only the evangelical Right roots its policies in scripture and bases its platforms on the Bible. And while

---

188 White House press conference, August 21, 2019
189 Christian Broadcasting Network CBN News January 30, 2019
190 Twitter @parscale April 30, 2019
191 House of Representatives floor debate, December 18, 2019
192 Paula White sermon, The River Church, Tampa Florida, June 2019
193 Presidential inauguration Ceremony, January 20, 2017 in Washington, DC
194 The New Yorker, "Franklin Graham's Uneasy Alliance with Donald Trump" –Eliza Griswold, September 11, 2018

Franklin Graham has enjoyed VIP access to the Trump-era evangelical power grab, he declared on Facebook that secular Americans constitute a greater domestic threat than the whole of our global adversaries.

 Franklin Graham
December 27, 2019 · 🌐

What is the most serious threat facing America as we come to a new year? Cyber attacks from China? North Korea's nuclear capabilities? A new cold war with Russia? The ongoing fight against Islamic terrorists? All of these are very significant threats. However, the biggest threat to America is not from outside nations—it's from within. The United States is the most blessed nation on earth. And that is because our forefathers gave us a foundation based on God and His Word. The biggest threat to our country's future is that we turn our back on God and have His hand of blessing removed.

Franklin's message is, "Forget ISIS. The seculars are a-comin' for your freedoms. It's a war on Christ!" (Joshua Feuerstein would be proud.)

I need to clarify something. I reject the claims made by my former religion, and I'm a vocal critic of the Bible, the indoctrination of children, religious shaming, state/church overreach, and magical thinking. As an activist I am waged in a battle, but it's an ideological one, a battle to see the best ideas win the day. For those best ideas to prevail, wrong or destructive ideas must be targeted. As Robert Green Ingersoll so eloquently said, "The more false we destroy, the more room we make for the true."[195] Ingersoll also said that "The liberty of a man is not safe in the hands of any church."[196]

Christian nationalists want the privilege of operating beyond any zone of criticism. Some of the more indignant zealots seem to crave an American version of Pakistan's blasphemy laws, which forbid derogatory remarks against Islam or Allah under dire penalty. Yet the very notion of an unquestionable faith, claim, or idea is an anathema to

---

195 Robert G. Ingersoll "Orthodoxy" 1884
196 Robert G. Ingersoll "Some Mistakes of Moses" Section III 1879

---

true liberty, and American Christians shouldn't get preferential treatment every time they cry foul.

Is there genuine persecution of Christians in our world? Absolutely, just as there is genuine persecution of Jews, Muslims, Hindus, Buddhists, Sikhs, atheists, and in any instance where one tribe wishes to dominate another. These acts of oppression, torture, murder, and genocide are repugnant to all moral creatures. But it's repulsive for unrepressed American Christians to invoke the Armenian Genocide, the Third Reich, and ISIS beheadings to fortify their local perches of entitlement. They invoke true atrocity to sell panic about an imaginary threat to liberty.

For example, Fox News columnist Douglas MacKinnon constantly stokes fears about imminent liberal persecution, asking "How Long Will I Be Allowed to Remain a Christian?"[197] The National Review warns of "campaigns of legal and social harassment" against American Christians.[198] The Christian Post predicts a "coming of persecution for American Christians."[199] Televangelist Jim Bakker frets that a democratic presidential victory in 2020 would result in American Christians being murdered in the streets.[200]

Yet these evangelicals shouting from the tops of their high mountains aren't being dragged to a colosseum execution by the Roman Empire. They're merely being required to share their abundance with others, and they are—finally—starting to be held constitutionally accountable. They are being disagreed with. Challenged. Contradicted.

In a truly free nation, religions should be—they must be—contradicted. With the rising of the nones, these challenges will occur more and more, Christian nationalists will become increasingly desperate, and like a cornered animal, they will flail and bite and claw and shout.

---

197 Fox News "How Long Will I Be Allowed to Remain a Christian?" Douglas MacKinnon, April 21, 2018
198 National Review "The Coming Test Acts Will Challenge Religious Freedom" January 21, 2019
199 The Christian Post "The Coming of Persecution for American Christians" July 24, 2019
200 The Jim Bakker Show June 19, 2019

They'll sermonize about disobedience, despotism, and divine wrath. They'll invoke history's greatest monsters. They'll grumble about permissiveness and moral anarchy. They'll fabricate stories about the Founding Fathers. They'll huff at the Other—those different from them who demand equal treatment, equal rights, equal opportunities, and equal representation. The pious will warn of hellfire, and they'll likely continue to sell their proverbial souls for any promise of privilege.

George Orwell famously wrote in his masterwork *1984* that "No one ever seizes power with the intention of relinquishing it." Hence the flop sweat of America's theocrats as their sands trickle down the hourglass. They're being opposed in a battle of ideas, the kind of battle encouraged in a free republic within the framework of the Constitution, and a necessary struggle to restore the values and intent of our founders.

> In every country and in every age, the priest has been hostile to liberty. He is always in alliance with the despot, abetting his abuses for protection to his own. It is error alone that needs the support of government. Truth can stand by itself.
> —Thomas Jefferson[201]

---

201 Thomas Jefferson to Horatio G. Spafford, March 17, 1814

CHAPTER SEVEN:

Out of My Cold, Dead Hands: America's Love Affair with Guns

IN MARCH 2019 I was invited to speak at an outdoor Atheist Day rally at the State Capitol grounds in Austin, Texas. Most of the presenters were addressing state/church separation and the rise of America's non-religious voting bloc.

As I waited for my turn at the microphone, I noticed a group of men lingering near the periphery of the crowd, men who looked quite out of place for an Atheist Day assembly. I focused my eyes toward them. I counted nine people between the approximate ages of twenty and sixty, many of them wearing military clothing, most packing firearms, including one AR-15 slung over a shoulder. Two men held a large banner bearing the phrase *Don't Tread On Me*. All were white.

One of my colleagues engaged them to find out what was happening. This small group had assembled at the State Capitol in protest of Texas's vote on new gun safety initiatives. House Bill (HB) 316 promoted suicide prevention and a public campaign for safe gun storage. HB 1207 would require prompt reporting of lost or stolen guns. HB 1208 would create a path where county courts could force the surrender of weapons. HB 1236 would ban even legal firearms on college campuses. HB 2280 would allow for clear signage by business owners forbidding handguns in stores and offices.

Apparently this small band of demonstrators felt that these bills, which seemed perfectly reasonable, were an assault on their individual liberties and a violation of the U.S. Constitution's Second Amendment. *Don't Tread On Me.*

The Second Amendment remains one of the most hotly debated issues in the United States, and the arguments themselves reveal how deeply guns are embedded in American notions about freedom and liberty. The Second Amendment of the Constitution declares, "A well-regulated Militia, being necessary to the security of a free State, the right of the people to keep and bear Arms, shall not be infringed."

America has long cradled its firearms, with more guns than citizens. Handguns. Shotguns. Rifles. Semi-automatics. Fully automatics. More than 11 million new firearms are manufactured every year, not including those made for the military.[202] I'm included in U.S. gun statistics; I have two pistols of my own.

There are a lot of misconceptions about American gun owners, the laziest one lumping all into a giant, rusty pickup truck with a Confederate flag flapping from the antenna. The Internet is loaded with videos of unqualified, reckless, or outright dangerous people pulling the trigger on some unfortunate outcome, and while those alarming examples do exist, they often have the effect of drawing the Big Picture in caricature. It seems unfathomable to many, but there's a huge swath of gun owners that abhors violence, received proper firearms training, uses every safety precaution, and treats deadly weapons with the care and respect they deserve. Their guns are for recreation and/or for home protection, in controlled environments, purchased legally, and handled with temperance. Many gun owners even refuse to hunt, opting for paper targets at a local shooting range.

And—believe it or not—many American gun owners hate the National Rifle Association.

---

202 Small Arms Survey June 2018

I was thirty years old when the NRA knighted its newest leader, the legendary actor Charlton Heston. Heston's Hollywood résumé was long and distinguished, with his most famous roles in big-budget Bible epics like *Ben Hur* and *The Ten Commandments*. When I first saw *The Ten Commandments* on my parents' modest television as a teenager, I was blown away, and Charlton Heston's Moses remains my favorite version of the character. No doubt Heston's on-screen nobility informed the public perception of him, and he carried his film image as emancipator into his political life.

A former political lefty, Charlton Heston had become disenfranchised with the Democratic Party, switching to Republican in the 1980s and becoming a fierce campaigner for President Ronald Reagan, Bush I, and Bush II. His activism also coincided with conservative concerns about a shift in American culture.

The 1980s saw a lot of pulpit-pounding about the moral decline of a generation. Immoral songs on the radio. Immoral films in the theaters. Immoral shows on the television. Immoral books in the retail stores. The rise of progressivism. The growing influence of non-Christians. Religious/political organizations such as the Moral Majority fretted about the national assault on "traditional values." Tipper Gore's Parents Music Resource Center was demanding parental advisory stickers on explicit albums to protect children. And American Christians had spun themselves into hysterics about Satanic influence in music, movies, television, games, toys, and even cartoons. I described this Satanic Panic in my 2017 speech at the Orlando, Florida, Freethought Conference, easily found on YouTube.[203]

Charlton Heston was outraged about the slippery slope of permissiveness being foisted onto a once-great nation. He publicly (rightly) denounced the 1992 Ice-T song "Cop Killer"[204] as a contemptuous attempt to sell shock to the American people. Against the outcry, Ice-T pulled the song from the album. In 1997 Heston (wrongly) told an

203 Florida Freethought Conference 2017, Seth Andrews "The Satanic Panic: The Witch Hunt of the Late Twentieth Century (YouTube)
204 Time Warner Shareholder Meeting July 1992

audience at the Free Congress Foundation that God-fearing, white, straight, heterosexual, gun owners were being persecuted by liberals via "cultural warfare." Defending the Second Amendment three years later at Brandeis University in Massachusetts, he (laughably) aligned gun-control advocates with McCarthyism and proclaimed that "Political correctness is tyranny with manners."

Moses had spoken. God despised liberals. God loved the NRA.

The National Rifle Association was founded in 1871 "to promote and encourage rifle shooting on a scientific basis."[205] The focus was competitive marksmanship and proper safety training. The NRA was created partly as a response to Civil War statistics that showed that Union soldiers had been startlingly bad at hitting their enemy targets. Simply, they couldn't shoot straight.[206] Rifle ranges were established, and riflemen set to honing their skills.

Throughout the early to mid-twentieth century, various gun regulations were installed by the federal government in response to the growing gun culture. The Tommy gun gangsters of the 1930s inspired federal regulation of machine guns,[207] and the assassinations of President John Kennedy, Malcolm X, Robert Kennedy, and Dr. Martin Luther King prompted the Omnibus Crime Control And Safe Streets Act and the Gun Control Act of 1968, significantly restricting gun sales and shoring up the protocols for licensing a firearm.

In the 1980s gun violence seared itself into public debate. President Ronald Reagan was shot and wounded by John Hinckley, Jr., in 1981, White House Press Secretary James Brady had been permanently disabled with a bullet to the head, and incidents of gun violence surged among the population throughout the 1980s and early 1990s, peaking in 1993.[208]

---

205 National Rifle Association website, "A Brief History of the NRA"
206 Washington Post "Timeline of the NRA" January 12, 2013
207 National Firearms Act 1934
208 U.S. Department of Justice Special Report "Firearm Violence, 1993–2011"

Amid growing public concerns about gun violence and the institution of stricter gun laws (required background checks, a ten-year federal ban on assault weapons, etc.), the National Rifle Association got political, and its primary weapon for opposing gun restrictions was the Second Amendment, a tool waved proudly by NRA front men such as Charlton Heston. The NRA and many American gun owners framed the gun debate under the larger umbrella of personal liberty, freedom, and constitutionally protected, God-ordained rights. Muzzle the gun, and you muzzle the citizen. Restrict the gun, and you restrict the owner. Outlaw the gun, and you criminalize the American and defy God. The very idea of increased firearms restrictions was resisted as oppression. *Don't Tread On Me.* This attitude was perhaps best represented on bumper stickers and T-shirts bearing the words "I'll give you my gun when you pry it from my cold, dead hands."

Charlton Heston himself used the "cold dead hands" line on several occasions, including his NRA retirement speech in 2003. On that last day, Heston held a rifle above his head in defiance as the adoring crowd cheered. The moment was uniquely "American," and his defiant war cry echoes today.

Large-scale gun violence has become a common American headline. The year 1999 saw the murder of thirteen students by two fellow classmates at Columbine High School in Colorado, and the United States began down the tragic road of the normalized mass shooting, including the following :

- 32 dead and 17 wounded on the campus of Virginia Tech (April 16, 2007)

- 18 people—including U.S. House Representative Gabrielle Giffords—shot in Tucson, Arizona (January 8, 2011)

- 12 slain and 58 wounded at an Aurora, Colorado, movie theater (July 20, 2012)

- The Sandy Hook Elementary School massacre of 20 kids (December 14, 2012)

- 49 killed and 53 wounded in an Orlando gay nightclub (June 12, 2016)

- 58 killed and 851 injured by a mass shooter in Las Vegas (October 1, 2017)

- 17 dead, 17 wounded at Marjory Stoneman Douglas High School in Parkland, Florida (February 14, 2018)

After the August 4, 2019, mass shooting in Dayton, Ohio, killing nine and injuring seventeen, Fox News host Sean Hannity offered his own solution to America's mass shooting problem: more guns. On the day after the murders, Hannity proposed that schools and retailers surround their facilities with ex-police and retired military personnel. "They should be on every floor of every school." Hannity suggested that we compensate these armed guards by exempting them from income, state, and federal taxes. He had suggested a similar plan in 2018 after the Parkland shooting. Hannity rebuffed all notions of gun reform as an infringement "on the rights of hundreds of millions of Americans."[209]

This "good guy with a gun" reasoning was ostensibly validated on December 28, 2019, after Keith Thomas Kinnunen opened fire at West Freeway Church of Christ in White Settlement, Texas, and was shot dead by the church's head of security. Two parishioners had been killed, but gun advocates declared that things could have been much worse, and they rallied around the Texas case as a real-world example proving the necessity of protective firearms.

Strangely, nobody seemed interested in the larger question surrounding that tragic day: why would a house of omnipotent God require armed security, and why did God not protect his own children against the evil assassin? Deuteronomy 31:6 promises "He will never leave you or forsake you." Isaiah 54:17 proudly proclaims to the faithful that "no weapon formed against you shall prosper." Psalm 46:1 calls God "our refuge and strength, an ever-present help in trouble." The

---

209 Fox News "Sean Hannity" August 4, 2019

New Testament book of 2 Thessalonians promises that "the Lord is faithful, and he will strengthen you and protect you from the evil one."[210]

I'm not trying to build a soapbox upon the caskets of the dead, but I feel compelled to examine the contradictory notions of 1) divine protection and 2) the carrying of guns for personal defense. The biblical god has unlimited ability, as declared in Jeremiah 32:17: "Ah, Sovereign LORD, you have made the heavens and the earth by your great power and outstretched arm. Nothing is too hard for you." God's children rest in the cradle of his embrace and are commanded, "Do not be anxious about anything, but in every situation, by prayer and petition, with thanksgiving, present your requests to God. And the peace of God, which transcends all understanding, will guard your hearts and your minds in Christ Jesus." (Philippians 4:6-7)

Contrast pulpit proclamations about protection and peace against the rampant fear that seems to permeate Christian culture. Believers lay claim to God's "ever-present help in trouble,"[211] even as they lock their doors, install their home alarm systems, monitor their security cameras, prime their mace cans, and load their concealed firearms. The divinely protected avoid the dark alley, the stranger, the sketchy situation. Despite the lofty talk about ever-present help, they warily behave as if calamity could strike at any moment. For all practical purposes, they act like nonbelievers.

The contradictions continue among gun advocates who trumpet the global superiority of their great nation and its military while simultaneously warning that they might someday have to revolt against it. They brandish their guns as a safety measure against tyranny. In March 2018, National Rifle Association liaison Shannon Alford said as much to *USA Today*: "The Second Amendment is not about hunting. It is not about competitive shooting. The Second Amendment is about self-defense. It's about being able to stop people who would

---

210 2 Thessalonians 3:3-5
211 Psalm 46:1

do you harm, whether that's a criminal or the government."[212] Alford spoke in advance of the national March For Our Lives rallies, anti-gun demonstrations organized by surviving students of the Parkland shooting. The rallies drew more than two million participants.[213] In response National Rifle Association television host Grant Stinchfield called the protesters "radicals with a history of violent threats, language, and actions,"[214] further propagating the claim that gun control advocates, and even victims, were dangerous to American liberty. These sentiments are echoes of politicians such as Oklahoma Senator Tom Coburn, who declared, "The Second Amendment wasn't written so you can go hunting. It was to create a force to balance a tyrannical force here."[215]

It's a strange rallying cry: *The United States is the greatest nation. And we have to protect ourselves from it!*

As an exercise, let's allow that the militia crowd has a valid argument. Let's decide that everyday citizens might someday have to rise up in arms against their own government after a coup. Let's accept the claim that the president and both houses of Congress would collude in tyranny against the whole of the American population, and that 1.2 million active military men and women would then follow suit, denying all conscience, turning on their American brothers and sisters, and gliding into lockstep as revolutionaries. Even if those ridiculous ideas were true, the common American gun owner would face absolute extermination. These small bands of armchair warriors would discharge their puny Glocks and Remingtons into a billions-of-dollars blitzkrieg of war technology that could melt whole nations to glass. They'd make George Custer look like General William Halsey. Their defeat would be quick, humiliating, and total.

What drives this lousy argument in defense of firearms? I'm not

---

212 USA Today "For Many Americans, the Second Amendment is a Defense Against Their Own Government" March 22, 2018
213 Newsweek "More than 2 Million in 90 Percent of Voting Districts Joined March For Our Lives Protests" March 26, 2018
214 NRATV, March 21, 2018
215 New York Times "Senator Unveils Bill to Limit Semiautomatic Arms" January 24, 2013

clairvoyant, but I can assess the disposition and claims of the NRA crowd, and I can crawl back into the attitudes of my youth with some objectivity.

My parents had guns in the home, but we weren't avid shooters. My father and I would occasionally target soda cans with his .22 rifle, and he owned a .410 shotgun. Mother had a small-caliber handgun hidden in her bedroom closet, but I never saw her carry a pistol until she took one out of her purse to show it off about fifteen years ago. It was unloaded (she was nervous about accidental discharge), and I stared blankly as she fumbled for over a minute to find the stray bullets tumbling around the bottom of her handbag. (Apparently, her gun would come in handy if she were ever mugged by a sloth.) At the time, she was a retired woman in her sixties, but she had long supported personal firearms for protection. Her world always seemed a dangerous one, and she felt empowered by the hardware. Her gun was also a statement, a defiant demonstration of her Second Amendment liberties. For many years, I assumed her attitude on the subject.

For just a moment let's go back in time to examine American firearms during the time that the Second Amendment was instituted. Let's assess an eighteenth-century framework for "a well-related militia."

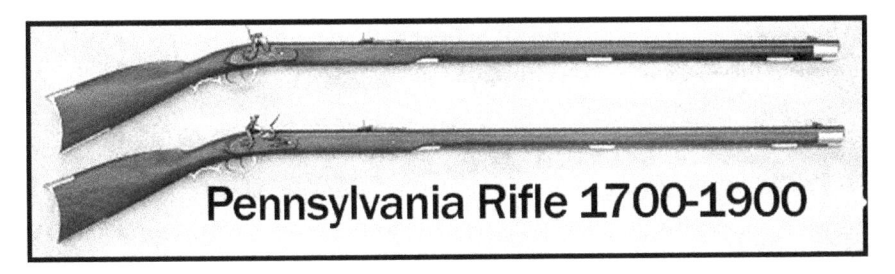

Pennsylvania Rifle 1700-1900

Image: Wikipedia

It was the time of the Revolutionary War. It was the time of the Pennsylvania Long Rifle, the famed firearm of pioneer Daniel Boone. Before every pull of the trigger, black powder would be poured from a horn into a charger, and the bullet—a lead ball the size of a pea—would be wrapped in a greased patch and rammed down the barrel. Loading was difficult, and the powder often clogged the barrel. The wooden stocks were known to break on heavy impact. Early versions of the Pennsylvania Rifle managed approximately one shot per minute. Maximum effective range was three hundred yards.[216]

Revolutionary War
Flintlock Pistol

Image: iStockPhoto

The flintlock pistol was a clumsy handgun with a twelve-inch barrel. Firing required a piece of flint that had to be sparked to ignite the powder. The guns were terribly inaccurate, and they were prone to misfire. The long loading process usually allowed only one shot during a close-quarters firefight before hand-to-hand combat became necessary.

These examples provide two snapshots of America's early gun technology. Certainly the Founding Fathers couldn't have imagined anything like the modern-day AR-15, which fires forty-five rounds per minute at a muzzle velocity of more than three thousand feet per second. Also, colonial militias existed during a fluid and volatile time in America's history as Great Britain waged war against this new nation, but those militias remained accountable to the Massachusetts

---

216 American Military Shoulder Arms, Volume 1: "Colonial and Revolutionary War Arms" George D. Moller 2011

Provisional Congress Committee of Safety and the umbrella authority of government.[217] They were not intended to unleash autonomous farmers pointing rifles toward fellow citizens at their own discretion.

In America's recent history, hate groups such as the Ku Klux Klan have used the "well-regulated militia" argument to justify white supremacy and the rejection of laws they consider un-American, often using gun violence to force minorities back into the shadows. The far-right militia group The Three Percenters is an anti-government organization founded during the tenure of President Barack Obama, its name referring to the 3 percent of American colonists who fought the British during the Revolutionary War. The Three Percenters reflect a common militia claim that Democratic presidents, left-wing radicals, and even the United Nations seek a New World Order, a world without borders or national sovereignty.[218] *The New York Times* published a February 12, 2018, profile of the Atomwaffen Division, a neo-Nazi organization linked to several murders across the U.S. *Atomwaffen* translates to "atomic weapons" in German. That organization claims that the United States government has already gone rogue, and it anoints itself a resistance force against the American oligarchy. Members of the Arkansas State Militia Corps pose in military camouflage and train for battle with paintball guns.[219] The scene would be comical if it wasn't so scary.

In fairness these are fringe groups, and again, many American gun owners aren't drinking the Kool-Aid of conspiracy, but they often share the militias' fears about progressive encroachment on their fierce nationalist notions, convinced that traitorous liberal foes must be resisted, even with force. For many, weapons like the AR-15 could back that resistance. But where does this conspiratorial thinking come from?

New York University published an interesting 2008 study by several renowned psychologists from NYU, Berkeley, Cambridge, and the

---

217 "The Provincial Committees of Safety of the American Revolution" Western Reserve University, Agnes Hunt 1904
218 Southern Poverty Law Center "Antigovernment Movement"
219 Vice "An Up-Close Look at America's Evolving Militia Movement" Jen Osborne February 20, 2019

University of Texas at Austin titled "The Secret Lives of Liberals and Conservatives: Personality Profiles, Interaction Styles, and the Things They Leave Behind." The study examined the "psychological needs, motives, and orientations toward the world," and it revealed striking differences in how conservatives and liberals think and behave.

In the research, conservatives were usually more reserved, more attracted to in-group symbols such as flags and sports memorabilia, more organized, more structured, and less drawn to the chic and trendy. They also had a greater tendency toward xenophobia (the fear of outsiders), a trait that attracted many to the strong nationalist rhetoric of Donald Trump. Trump's America was one of protective walls and distrust of the immigrant. Trump attempted the Muslim ban and would consider registering Muslims in a national database.[220] His America was reflected in right-wing magazines such as *The New American*, which ran the story "Will Migrant Caravan Kill Your Child—With Disease?"[221] *Fox & Friends* host Brian Kilmeade helped propagate those fears by asking guest David Ward about possible danger. Ward replied, "They're coming in with diseases such as smallpox and leprosy and TB [tuberculosis] that are going to infect our people in the United States."[222] (Note: smallpox was globally eradicated by 1980.)

In his book *Sex, Power, and Partisanship*, psychologist Hector Garcia further explains that these insular, tribal tendencies are statistically more common among conservatives worldwide.

> Researchers found that conservatives in Spain hold more anti-Arab prejudice than liberals. A much larger study, called the Eurobarometer survey, assessed predictors of out-group prejudice in four thousand respondents across four European countries: the French were asked about the North Africans, Vietnamese, and Cambodians; the Dutch about Surinamers

220 Politifact "In Context: Donald Trump's Comments on a Database of American Muslims" November 24, 2015
221 New American "Will Migrant Caravan Kill Your Child—With Disease?" Selwyn Duke October 28, 2018
222 Fox & Friends October 29, 2018

and Turks; the Brits about West Indians, Indians, and Pakistani; and predictors **political conservatism** was the major predictor of out-group prejudice.[223]

Garcia goes on to reveal that conservatives tend to be more germophobic than liberals and are more easily disgusted by things that exist beyond their established norms—everything from exotic foods to sexual behaviors to spiders to foreigners. Garcia's book explores possible genetic causes for this impulse toward disgust, and it's a hugely revelatory journey into the forces fueling America's two major political ideologies.

This much is certain: One camp is more prone to experiencing a fear of the Other.

The National Rifle Association has deftly targeted those fears. The NRA spent more than $5 million on lobbying in 2017.[224] That same year official spokesperson Dana Loesch appeared in an NRA video ad accusing gun opponents as being national saboteurs who, "slashing away with their leaks and sneers, their phony accusations and gagging sanctimony, drive their daggers through the heart of our future."[225] Loesch finished the ad by predicting that liberals' "fate will be failure, and they will perish in the political flames of their own fires." A February 2018 ad showed Dana Loesch turning an hourglass, the spilling sands sending the clear message to anti-gun Americans: "Your time is running out." These implied threats played quite well to paranoid gun owners.

The good news? The National Rifle Association's efforts to block responsible new gun legislation seems to be waning against public opinion. *Politico* recently reported internal conflict at the NRA.[226] The organization's president, Oliver North, was ousted in early 2019 after

223 Sex, Power, and Partisanship: How Evolutionary Science Makes Sense of Our Political Divide Hector Garcia 2019
224 Center for Responsive Politics, Senate Office of Public Records April 24, 2018
225 NRATV June 2017
226 Politico "'I'm Worried': Allies Fear NRA Has Lost Its Power In Washington" August 16, 2019

an extortion scheme that took place on his watch. The NRA was revealed to have ties to Maria Butina, the Russian agent convicted of infiltrating American gun rights groups. Several NRA board members resigned in August 2019 over reports of mismanagement and lavish spending. A recent Fox News poll (go figure) revealed a negative public opinion rating for the first time in NRA history.[227] Half of all U.S. states passed at least one gun-control measure in 2018.[228]

Yet the NRA's influence (and the "guns versus tyranny" narrative) bleeds—literally—into the twenty-first century as the organization aggressively lobbies to block further research and data on gun violence.[229]

Perhaps you find me a hypocrite. I've already admitted to owning firearms and keeping them in my home. I've received firearms training, I target shoot, and although the prospect grieves me greatly, I'm prepared to use lethal force against a home intruder. But my guns aren't part of my national identity or my human one, and I'm not threatened by proposals that could potentially reduce the whiz of lethal bullets in this country. I resist all claims that a government unable to agree on the basics—same-sex marriage, abortion, immigration, climate change, the economy, the military, foreign policy—could ever sync into a unified oppression of its own people. And I'm heartbroken about those slain in the streets, the schools, the nightclubs, the churches, the culture, almost forty thousand U.S. gun victims every single year.[230]

It's a messy situation. The eight-hundred-pound gorilla is well out of its cage, and the ubiquity of guns is a problem not soon solved. Gun advocates have a valid point when they protest that mental health is a factor in some gun homicides and that stricter gun laws will have no effect on criminals who ignore the laws, restricting only the law-abiding. Gun opponents have a valid point when they reveal that

227 Fox News "Fox News Poll: Most Back Gun Restrictions After Shootings, Trump Ratings Down" Dana Blanton August 14, 2019
228 Giffords Law Center Annual Report "Gun Law Trend Watch: 2018 Year-End Review"
229 NPR "How the NRA Worked to Stifle Gun Violence Research" April 5, 2018
230 Pew Research Center "What the Data Says About Gun Deaths in the U.S." August 16, 2019

mental-health issues aren't precursors for violent behavior and don't result in equivalent gun violence in other nations. Anti-gun advocates also correctly note that fewer overall firearms would statistically result in fewer gun incidents and that there's no good reason for civilians to possess military-grade assault weapons. This position becomes even more compelling against the fact that most weapons used in U.S. mass shootings were obtained legally.[231]

At the very least, we can—and should—embrace these realities: The United States has more guns per capita than any other country.[232] Gun homicide rates are 25 percent higher in the U.S. than in other wealthy countries.[233] The United States has the second-highest number of global mass shooters, surpassed only by Yemen.[234] Modern weapons were developed several centuries after the writing of the Second Amendment. And as the March For Our Lives demonstrates, the American population is increasingly desperate to put a stop to the carnage, even if it means surrendering its guns in the name of public safety.

Beyond the logistics, it's time for Americans to evolve past the paranoid attitudes that fuel much of the gun culture—expanding their horizons, dropping their guard, having a little more faith in their fellow human beings, and adopting a more xenophilic attitude toward those of different political parties, races, cultures, religions, and borders.

Yes, there are dangerous people platforming dangerous ideas. Yes, we must be vigilant. But there are so many instances of tribal isolation and unfounded fears that it seems obvious that the whole world could see much clearer from a more charitable vantage. We are all part of the diverse, fragile, precious human condition, and unfounded paranoia only compounds the divisions between us.

---

231 Statista "Number of Mass Shootings in the United States Between 1982 and December 2019, by Legality of Shooter's Weapons" December 12, 2019
232 Small Arms Survey 2018
233 OECD, WHO, American Journal of Medicine, Grinshteyn and Hemenway, 2010
234 Adam Lankford, University of Alabama, Small Arms Survey 2015

CHAPTER EIGHT:

Traitors in our Midst: Patriotism and Protest When America Goes to War

"THANK YOU FOR your service." This is a common expression of gratitude by American citizens toward their military. I spoke those words when I was a conservative Christian, and I speak them today. I've been fortunate enough to have enjoyed rights and privileges hard won and protected by soldiers past and present, and I understand how lucky I am.

When I turned eighteen, I was required by law to register with Selective Service for the draft, but I was fortunate to reach adulthood during a time of relative global peace. Unlike the young men of the Civil War, the Great War, the Nazi threat, and Vietnam, my late-teenage self was relatively unconcerned with the world beyond my own borders. I'd never traveled abroad. I lived in the safe cocoon of the Christian heartland. My biggest worries were finding a job, getting a car, and navigating the dating scene. In school I'd gotten the Cliffs Notes about history's major conflicts, but my attitudes about United States military action reflected a staunch conservative upbringing and notions of national superiority. My country was God's country.

A popular T-shirt slogan says, "If you can't stand behind our troops, feel free to stand in front of them." This was my disposition toward all

U.S. military action. A citizen could disagree and debate *before* the first shots of any conflict were fired, but once the shooting started, the good patriot would line up in support of America's soldiers without question. In my Republican sphere, there was much talk about our military heroes, and even those who'd served uneventful time in the army, navy, air force, or marines were automatically elevated several rungs in the consciousness of the American conservative. These men and women were prepared to answer the call, to enter the danger zone, to risk everything for the sake of security and freedom.

Many American soldiers have paid dearly with their lives and limbs, navigating dangers that most civilians can't even imagine. Their commitment and sacrifice can't be overstated, and much about the military hero narrative remains true. Yet it is not the whole story.

In 1968—the year of my birth—the Vietnam War claimed the lives of more than 16,000 Americans, almost 28,000 South Vietnamese, and approximately 200,000 North Vietnamese soldiers.[235] I was seven the year that war ended, and I was a teenager before I had even casual conversations about Vietnam, those discussions broad and ignorant. I couldn't even find Vietnam on a map. I didn't know why the United States had fought. I didn't understand the history or culture of the enemy. I was oblivious to the definition or implications of communism beyond religious history lessons that linked it to the devil. I considered war protesters the poster children of a weak and often treasonous Left that refused to stand under the American flag. I grouped together the veteran, the anthem, and the noble nation "under God." To question one was to question it all.

In my limited understanding, I believed that the United States had lost the Vietnam War simply because it had failed to properly commit. Had we scaled the war machine appropriately, our forces—with the anti-communist God on our side—could have leveled the North Vietnamese Army. America had fallen victim to its own half-measures.

---

235 National Archives Military Records "Vietnam War U.S. Military Fatal Casualty Statistics" archives.gov

We should have unleashed the whirlwind. Blown the north to dust. Obliterated all resistance with the fearsome might at our disposal. There are many conservatives who believe this same thing today.

I wish I could introduce my younger self to Vietnam War Marine Corporal John Musgrave of Fairmont, Missouri, who served with the Third Marine Division in 1967 at the age of eighteen. Musgrave hadn't been drafted. He had volunteered for duty. He loved his country. He wanted to be an active rifle in America's battle to liberate a nation. His 1st Battalion was assigned to Con Thien near the Vietnamese Demilitarized Zone (DMZ), a strategically critical camp known by marines as Leatherneck Square, and a meat grinder so assailed by enemy fire that soldiers had nicknamed it the Dead Marine Zone.[236] In the muddy, bloody throes of combat, John Musgrave's disdain for the enemy was absolute: "My hatred for them was pure. Pure. I hated them so much. And I was so scared of them. Boy, I was terrified of them. And the scareder [sic] I got, the more I hated them."[237]

When Musgrave first killed a North Vietnamese Army (NVA) soldier in battle, he drowned in guilt. He had taken the life of another human being, and he faced a long tour of duty where he might have to kill again and again. The taking of human life grieved him to his marrow.

After watching a fellow marine shredded to bits by a mine, John Musgrave rationalized his way through the doubts with an attitude long used by one tribe against another. In the Ken Burns and Lynn Novick documentary film *The Vietnam War*, Musgrave described the moment when he decided that the enemy soldiers weren't actually people:

> I said, "I will never kill another human being as long as I'm in Vietnam. However, I will waste as many *gooks* as I can find. I'll wax as many *dinks* as I can find. I'll smoke as many *zips*

---

236 "U.S. Marines in Vietnam: Fighting the North Vietnamese" Gary Telfer, 1984, Marine Corps Vietnam Operational Historical Series
237 Documentary The Vietnam War: A Film by Ken Burns and Lynn Novick Season 1, Episode 5

---

as I can find. But I ain't gonna kill anybody. You turn a subject into an object. It's Racism 101."

As he dodged NVA bullets in Con Thien, Musgrave had heard only echoes about the anti-war peace movement taking place back in the United States, those morsels of information usually coming from *Stars and Stripes*, the official magazine of the American military, a publication that claimed editorial independence but was produced inside the Department of Defense. From those carefully crafted articles, John gleaned his opinion about the war protesters: "I hated them before I ever knew anything about them."[238] Those "hippies" were opposing their own military. Betraying their own country. Aiding the enemy.

On November 7, 1967, John Musgrave's company was ambushed. He was shot in the jaw and then in the chest. The hole in his torso was inches wide. Fellow marines—several of whom were shot in the effort—dragged his critically wounded body out of the firefight. Musgrave was passed over in triage several times. His ribs had been shattered. His lung was pierced. Critical nerves had been severed. A doctor summoned the chaplain. His was a lost cause, a waste of time and resources. Finally, one of the surgeons intervened, emergency surgery was performed, and against the odds, John Musgrave survived his wounds.

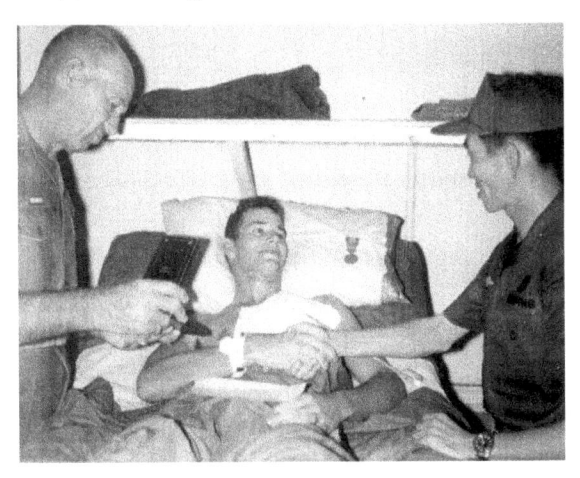

Photo courtesy of John Musgrave

---

238 Documentary The Vietnam War: A Film by Ken Burns and Lynn Novick Season 1, Episode 5

Returning to the United States after seventeen months inside various Navy hospitals, John was introduced firsthand to the best and worst of America's peace movement, a movement populated mostly by liberals and often on college campuses, a movement that had begun years earlier and split national opinion.

At the time Musgrave was shot, half a million American service personnel had been committed to Vietnam, with more than 35,000 U.S. soldiers dead and more than 100,000 wounded.[239] That same year, civil rights figures such as Dr. Martin Luther King, Jr., began publicly opposing the war on moral grounds, and thousands of like-minded protesters joined in across the nation. Public unrest about the war swelled. Some 400,000 anti-war demonstrators marched in New York City on April 15, 1967, and the following year on August 28, protesters rioted with local, state, and federal law enforcement officers outside the halls of the Democratic National Convention in Chicago. Footage of police officers brutally beating unarmed protesters with fists and billy clubs was broadcast nationally. Bodies were thrown through plate glass windows. Tear gas suffocated the crowds. *Washington Post* columnist Mary McGrory wrote "The streets literally ran with blood."[240]

This scenario would be repeated in the coming years, the most famous example being the May 4, 1970, shooting of unarmed college kids at Kent State University in Ohio. That massacre saw twenty-eight National Guard soldiers kill four students and wound nine others, with one victim permanently paralyzed.

These clashes reflected fierce national discontent and polarization—a Divided States of America. In the wake of this unrest, John Musgrave steeled his spine against the protests. He was appalled at the anti-American swell against the cause for which he had almost died. He became a Marine recruiter in defense of his military and his country. In his mind, it was the patriotic thing to do.

---

239 United States Army in Vietnam: The Final Years, 1965 – 1973 Jeffrey J. Clarke 1988, Center of Military History, Washington, DC
240 The Washington Post "The Chicago We'd Like To Forget" Mary McGrory, August 18, 1996

Yet John was being challenged by the difficult questions posed to him about the war in Vietnam, questions he often couldn't satisfactorily answer. So he began to ask questions of his own. He immersed himself in a fresh education about the justifications for and tactics within Vietnam. Increasingly, as he weighed the government's rationale for war against his own experiences and the terrible injuries and deaths of his fellow marines, Musgrave found himself recognizing hard truths, blanching at troublesome deceits, and increasingly doubtful about the whole operation. He soon disappeared within himself, shutting down outside interactions, numbing the pain with alcohol, driven to thoughts of suicide.

After President Richard Nixon engaged in the doublespeak of announcing troop withdrawals while ostensibly on course for military victory, John Musgrave shifted into quiet criticism of the Vietnam War. After the tragic killings of American students at Kent State, John could no longer remain quiet. He found his voice and became the very thing that he once despised: a war protester.

For the first time in U.S. history, military veterans were staging demonstrations against their own government. The year 1967 saw the founding of the nonprofit organization Vietnam Veterans Against the War (VVAW), which quickly swelled in membership to almost 25,000.[241] Soldiers stood shoulder to shoulder with the flower children of the Left in opposition to their government. The resistance shouted "Hell no; we won't go" and "Make love, not war." For this the protesters were called traitors.

In the safe cocoon of my twenties, had I seen an old 1968 photograph of John Musgrave demonstrating against his government during a time of war, I'd have winced with displeasure. As a "God and Country" conservative, I'd been patriotically primed to despise all war protesters, people such as actress Jane Fonda, dubbed "Hanoi Jane" for her 1972 tour of Vietnam where she publicly pled on North Vietnamese radio for the United States to halt its bombing and posed for photographs

---

241 A People's History of the Vietnam War Jonathan Neale, 2003

alongside a North Vietnamese anti-aircraft gun. (Note: In a recent HBO documentary, she apologized for the "thoughtless insulting of America's soldiers."[242])

Navy lieutenant John Kerry had been a swift boat commander in Vietnam before turning his energies against the war, taking a key leadership role with the VVAW. On April 22, 1971, Kerry spoke before the Senate Committee on Foreign Relations, accusing American soldiers of "crimes committed on a day-to-day basis" (rape, dismemberment, the murder of civilians, burning villages), those accusations repudiated by many of Kerry's fellow Vietnam War veterans who declared, "It didn't happen that way."[243] There were rampant rumors that Kerry received war medals for valor that he did not deserve, and those rumors shot into the spotlight when John Kerry became the 2004 Democratic candidate for president. Conservative talk radio bullhorns like Rush Limbaugh blasted Kerry for filming self-aggrandizing home movies of himself in the Vietnamese jungles.[244] On several occasions in 2004 Fox News's Sean Hannity hosted John O'Neill, member of the anti-Kerry political group "Swift Boat Veterans for Truth" (the Swifties) and coauthor of *Unfit for Command: Swift Boat Veterans Speak Out Against John Kerry*. The SBVT campaign against Kerry has been largely discredited, as "naval records and accounts from other sailors contradicted almost every claim they made,"[245] but at the time I was interested only in the accusations, not the refutations. In 2004, I still held a religious allegiance to the Republican Party.

Whatever might be true or false about Kerry's service in Vietnam, his caricature fed my notions about the American war protester, and it checked all the outrage boxes: Liar. Opportunist. Democrat. Traitor. My conviction was absolute. No true American would criticize his own nation during a time of war.

---

242 HBO documentary Jane Fonda in Five Acts 2018
243 Quote by Phil Gioia The Vietnam War: A Film by Ken Burns and Lynn Novick Season 1, Episode 9
244 Rush Limbaugh Radio Show March 22, 2004 "Kerry Fails War on Terror Test"
245 New York Times "Kerry Pressing Swift Boat Case Long After Loss" May 28, 2006

I was twenty-two when President George H. W. Bush waged Operation Desert Storm. I was thirty-three when his son George W. Bush initiated post 9/11 attacks against the Taliban in Afghanistan before expanding the war into Iraq over "weapons of mass destruction." Across these various conflicts, I'd seen the televised footage of anti-war demonstrators and set my jaw against them. In my mind, once American triggers had been pulled, there was no place for disagreement. Lacing my allegiance was the happy-clappy jingoism that has become so familiar in conservative circles: "I Proudly Support Our Troops."

Today I still proudly support our troops, but not necessarily in the way that American conservatives demand.

In January 2020, *Psychology Today* posted an article by attorney and humanist activist David Niose titled "You've Been Conditioned for War." The article dropped on the heels of the U.S. drone strike against Iranian terrorist Qasem Soleimani and the spiking international tensions that followed. Niose observed how Americans have long been conditioned to align militarism with patriotism and how fear has so often been used to rally public support against enemies and perceived enemies. Our culture rightly thanks veterans for their service and honors them with military parades. Our televisions are filled with military recruitment ads. F-18 Hornets fly over football stadiums. The United States spends more on military defense than China, Saudi Arabia, India, France, Russia, Germany, and the United Kingdom combined[246] and has been in a near-constant state of war since the terrorist attacks of 9/11. The military is offered as a career opportunity for lifelong soldiers or the promise of college funding toward a job, attracting many poor and culturally disadvantaged young people without other prospects. There are more firearms than people in the United States, more than 390 million weapons constituting almost half of all civilian firearms worldwide.[247] Ours is the culture of the bullet, the shooting range, the gun show, and like our military,

---

246 Stockholm International Peace Research Institute, SIPRI Military Expenditure Database, April 2019
247 Small Arms Survey 2019

we're psychologically primed to fight guns with guns, some being military-style assault rifles such as the AR-15.

Those things represent strength, authority, and power in the minds of many American conservatives. That attitude once permeated my thinking, and my notions about the military often resembled religious dogmatism, a thought-stopping shield against anyone who dared to question. It was simply unfathomable that challenge or protest could be a genuinely patriotic act. It remains unfathomable to many Americans today.

Had Vietnam veteran John Musgrave's evolution from warrior to protester made him a traitor? Hadn't he, of all people, earned the right to question the senseless deaths of his fellow marines? To challenge America's motivations and tactics? To stand on the national stage for the purpose of saving human lives? Wasn't John Musgrave a true American patriot?

Had I once seen the out-of-context photograph of Musgrave—long-haired and thick-bearded—with his defiant fist in the air, I would have said "No," and I would have been terribly wrong.

1972 anti-war protest in Lawrence, Kansas. Photo courtesy of John Musgrave

My own opinions about Vietnam began to evolve after the release of Errol Morris's 2003 documentary film *The Fog of War: Eleven Lessons from the Life of Robert S. McNamara*. McNamara had served as U.S. Secretary of Defense from 1961 to 1968 and was a driving force for American escalation during the Vietnam War. He was so influential that the conflict was nicknamed McNamara's War, yet during his tenure under President Lyndon Johnson, McNamara's perceptions began to change. He soon privately lamented that the war itself was likely unwinnable.

Errol Morris's film was essentially an extension of McNamara's 1996 book *In Retrospect: The Tragedy and Lessons of Vietnam*, which included McNamara's candid admission that "political stability [in Vietnam] did not exist and was unlikely to ever be achieved." He'd admitted that the United States had entered the war without a proper understanding of the region, the nation, or the enemy. In the book, his regret was unmistakable: "We were wrong, terribly wrong. We owe it to future generations to explain why." At the time, McNamara also expressed concern that the lessons of Vietnam remained unheeded as the United States engaged in fresh conflicts abroad (it was the year of the 2003 Iraq invasion): "I do not believe that we should ever apply that economic, political, and military power unilaterally. If we had followed that rule in Vietnam, we wouldn't have been there."[248]

Perhaps most poignantly, Robert McNamara said these words before the camera: "War is so complex, it's beyond the ability of the human mind to comprehend. Our judgment, our understanding are not adequate. And we kill people unnecessarily."

When did so many Americans decide to absolve themselves of moral responsibility in matters of life and death? Why this blind allegiance to the commander in chief, the Defense Department, the generals who so often have been hammers who see all global problems as nails? Why does the Republican party so eagerly bang the drums of war without adequate consideration of the human costs? In a nation

---

248 Documentary The Fog of War: Eleven Lessons from the Life of Robert S. McNamara 2003

that claims a higher moral standard, wouldn't thoughtful, reverent consideration be the necessary, critical, patriotic act of all citizens? Should we not heed the wisdom of French statesman George Clemenceau, who once said, "War is too important a matter to be left to the military"?[249]

In the technological age—the drone age—we run the risk of being even more disconnected from the blood beyond the bombs. From the safety of our flat-screens, we see nondescript buildings explode, unnamed bridges destroyed, unrecognizable vehicles smashed, and anonymous people vaporized, and we shrug at the footage like we would at a video game. We watch a faceless Other disappear from the planet, and we shrug it off without regard for that person's history, family, hopes, dreams, potential, or value. Without true understanding, we glibly chalk up the statistic as a net gain for the human condition: The world is a safer place.

Gone is the somber reflection of Civil War Major General Robert E. Lee, who is reported to have said, "It is well that war is so terrible, or we should grow too fond of it."[250] Yes, Lee and his Confederate army needed to be battled and defeated for the liberation of slaves. Yes, the twentieth century's world wars were horribly necessary defenses against the tyranny of rogue nations. Yes, violent action is sometimes the required response against terrorists and the nations who enable them. Yes, war is sometimes unavoidable for virtue to prevail.

Yet we cannot ignore history. We cannot ignore the millions who have died in conflicts that might have—and should have—been avoided. We must not abstain from our patriotic duty to defend America's nobility, its conscience, its morality, its legacy. We must protect our own soldiers from needless suffering and death, and we must see beyond our own borders to the terrible costs also paid by the men, women, and children of foreign nations. We must approach the sobering implications of war, not with chest-pounding bravado,

---

249 As quoted in Soixante Anneés d'Histoire Française (1932) by Georges Suarez
250 Robert E. Lee: A Life Roy Blount Jr. 2006

---

but with a thoughtful, solemn consideration equal to the potential consequences so that—in unfortunate times when military force is required—our support of the soldiers stands solidly on a foundation of morality, sobriety, and wisdom.

Finally, whenever we observe our nation acting against its interests or our moral principles, we must exercise our patriotic duty to protest. Because it is healthy. Because human life is precious. Because we refuse to surrender our own minds. Because our government's notions about war have often proven fallible or false. And because we desperately want goodness to prevail.

> Yes, I was a marine, but I was first and foremost a citizen of the United States of America. And being a citizen, I have certain responsibilities. And the largest of those responsibilities is standing up to your government and saying 'no' when it's doing something that you think is not in this nation's best interests. That is the most important job that every citizen has. — John Musgrave, United States Marine Corps, Third Division[251]

For your bravery in battle and in patriotic protest, thank you, John, for your service.

---

251 Documentary The Vietnam War: A Film by Ken Burns and Lynn Novick Season 1, Episode 9

CHAPTER NINE:

An Eye for an Eye: American Justice and the Death Penalty

FAR-RIGHT CONSERVATIVE PUNDIT, attorney, and author Ann Coulter penned an April 14, 2014, column with an account of the botched execution of convicted killer Clayton Lockett, and she was delighted by it. Lockett, thirty-eight, had been sentenced to die by the state of Oklahoma after being convicted of murder, rape, sodomy, kidnapping, assault, and battery. His crimes had been unimaginably cruel. In 1999, when he was twenty-two, Lockett had kidnapped a nineteen-year-old named Stephanie Neiman, bound her, shot her multiple times with a twelve-gauge shotgun, and buried her alive in a shallow grave.

Sixteen years later, Lockett spent the better part of an hour writhing on the execution table. Thirty-four minutes into the execution, Lockett, who should have been unconscious from the start, lifted his head and in obvious pain said, "Something's wrong!" The attending doctor then realized that the phlebotomist had misplaced the IV and that the poor connection had failed to administer the proper dose of lethal drugs. With no more drugs available, he halted the procedure. While prison officials tried to decide what to do next, Clayton Lockett had a massive heart attack and died on the table.

Given the heinous nature of his crimes, it is difficult to have sympathy for Clayton Lockett. For Ann Coulter, sympathy wasn't a problem. She contrasted Lockett's abusive and brutal past with his paltry thirty-five minutes in the execution chamber, declaring, "Actually, I'm not that horrified. It sounds like he suffered a bit, which is nice, and he's dead, which was the objective of the whole enterprise."[252] Coulter blasted *The New York Times* for its critical reporting of the failings at Oklahoma State Penitentiary, asserting that "death penalty hysterics do not care about the victims of crime." She then lamented the lengthy and expensive appeals process for convicted murderers before suggesting that justice-seeking Americans could volunteer for firing squads to streamline the process. She finished, "I'd pay for the opportunity, especially if they promise my gun won't have a blank."

Twenty years ago, when I was a right-wing Christian, I might have joined her.

For all their talk about the sanctity of human life, many American Christians have an Old Testament sense of justice. My grandfather held a "string 'em up" attitude about convicted murderers. I have met conservatives who expressed admiration for Islamic nations that punish thieves with a machete to the wrist. The biblical reference to "eye for an eye" is carried out literally in Saudi Arabia. Wounding someone in the eye might result in a sentence of reciprocal eye gouging by authorities.[253] When criminals are flogged for breaking various local or national laws, their torture is met with pious ambivalence by the justice crowd.

Comedian Ron White famously joked that his home state of Texas was streamlining its capital punishment system by advancing the executions of murderers who had at least three eyewitnesses to their crimes. White said, "Other states are trying to abolish the death penalty. Mine's putting in an express lane." The audience cheered.

---

252 Ann Coulter, "Death Penalty Opponents, Have I Got a Deal for You!," May 14, 2014
253 Newsweek, "The World's Most Barbaric Punishments," July 8, 2010

From my more distant vantage, I can understand why the crowd was so enthusiastic about the execution of killers, and I completely understand why Stephanie Neiman's friends and family had no pity for Clayton Lockett. In Lockett's videotaped confession, his cold, matter-of-fact remorselessness chills the spine. Neiman had witnessed Lockett's break-in of a man's home, and Lockett decided not only to eliminate the witness but also first force her through a hell of torture that defies description. His execution wasn't mere justice; it was vengeance. An eye for an eye.

Contrast that notion with the story of Vicki Schieber. Schieber's daughter, Shannon, was brutally raped and murdered in 1998. The killer, Troy Graves, was arrested four years later, and authorities discovered that he had a long history of rape and assault.

However, Vicki Schieber, along with other victims she had contacted, decided not to seek the death penalty. Schieber became convinced that capital punishment was morally dubious, economically wasteful, unevenly applied, and a profound burden on the victims' families, as each death penalty conviction brings a mandated and often lengthy appeals process. (Graves was given the sentence of life without parole, which he is serving at the Colorado State Penitentiary.) Vicki Schieber is now an anti-death penalty activist, and she wants capital punishment eliminated nationwide.

Both camps, pro and con, make valid points.

Despite the common "string 'em up" mentality among binary thinkers, we can't escape the reality that there are monsters among us—those who are forever dangerous, who will never be rehabilitated, and who represent a net loss in the human moral equation. We can't forget the immeasurable pain of the victims and those they leave behind, and we shouldn't discount legitimate attempts at punitive equilibrium that require a life for a life. The message is compelling: if you murder a precious human being, you forfeit your right to exist. This is an attitude held by 55 percent of Americans, according to Pew

Research.[254] Rush Limbaugh and other Right-wing radio hosts fuel these fires with statements such as this one:

> Liberal opponents of capital punishment glibly argue that the death penalty provides no deterrent to the commission of capital crimes. Well, how on earth would we ever know? Only if we have swift and certain justice will we ever have an opportunity to test the deterrent effect of the death penalty.[255]

Limbaugh's message echoes Old Testament America: Quit pussyfooting, stop coddling criminals, nix all this courtroom nonsense, quickly exterminate the bad guys, and let's see how the murder rates react. This attitude reflects understandable frustration with a clogged legal system and, in many cases, a legitimate desire to give potential murderers a moment of pause while providing victims some semblance of justice.

I have had death penalty advocates ask me how I would react if my wife were horribly murdered, and I had difficulty responding. Others asked if I thought that Adolf Hitler would have deserved the electric chair, and I struggled to justify notions of clemency against his extermination of millions. If anyone deserved to be eradicated from this planet, Hitler did, and while I hold strong liberal views, I don't fall into the "all human life is precious" camp.

This is the hard reality: there are some people who bring only pain, destruction, and horror. They are a constant threat to public safety and a blight on the face of humanity, and—at least in theory—there is merit to the idea of removing them from the planet. If the killer suffers at the end, his suffering is a faint echo of the suffering he inflicted on others.

Those against capital punishment rightly protest a common conservative feed-them-to-the-lions mentality. I am reminded of the

---

254 Pew Research Center, "Shrinking Majority of Americans Support Death Penalty," March 28, 2014
255 Rush Limbaugh, The Way Things Ought to Be, 1992

homemade souvenir T-shirts sold outside the prison at serial killer Ted Bundy's 1989 execution.

Homemade shirt design from the 1989
prison demonstration at Ted Bundy's execution

The glee on the faces of the mob reflected the attitude many Americans had about Bundy's death in the electric chair. He had killed at least thirty young women and disqualified himself from the human race. As such, "moral" people rationalized treating his execution like sport, and without any reverence or reflection, the crowd cheered and waved banners as if they were at a football game. This vengeance-as-entertainment attitude is revealed in deeply troubling videos of the Bundy demonstrators.

Beyond notions of recreational killing or necessary justice lie serious concerns about the system. Pennsylvania State Senator Daylin Leach, a former criminal defense attorney, has joined Vicki Schieber in opposing capital punishment, repeatedly introducing anti-death penalty legislation in the Senate based on several points listed in a 2018 Joint State Government Commission Task Force report.[256] In summary the Commission found the following:

- Capital punishment is significantly more expensive than life sentences because of the mandatory appeals and lengthy overall process.

- Several condemnees had confirmed psychiatric problems unaddressed by the courts, meaning that states were executing mentally ill or "intellectually disabled" people.

- Some sentenced to death were exonerated of their crimes after the discovery of new evidence. How many genuinely innocent inmates have slipped through the cracks is unknown.

- The process is arbitrary, as race and ethnicity often play into the application of capital punishment, with racial bias often present within the communities where trials are held. According to the report, "In a very real sense, a given defendant's chance of having the death penalty sought, retracted, or imposed depends on where that defendant is prosecuted and tried."

- The objectivity of juries varies. Political bias, religious conviction, and a lack of education introduce potential problems with fairness.

- The quality of legal counsel is inconsistent. Many defense attorneys are simply ill-qualified to properly manage a death penalty case.

- There is no process for proportionality. Murderers in one case may receive death, while murderers in an identical, separate

---

256 Joint State Government Commission, "Capital Punishment in Pennsylvania: The Report of the Task Force and Advisory Committee," June 2018

case may get a prison sentence.

- Provision of county services to the victims is difficult to sustain over lengthy appeals, and the emotional toll to families is often compounded.

- The appeals process isn't consistent in readdressing evidence on death penalty cases.

- A Board of Pardons may unanimously recommend a governor pardon, but a governor's final decision is largely arbitrary.

- Research doesn't convincingly demonstrate that the fear of potential capital punishment deters homicide.

The Pennsylvania Committee's arguments are compelling, and they echo those of organizations such as Amnesty International, which invoked the case of Cameron Todd Willingham, a father who was executed in Texas for murdering his children before exonerating evidence was discovered.[257] Texas had killed an innocent man.

Out of the more than 1,500 executions in the United States in the last fifty years, how many of those inmates deserved a fresh look at the evidence? What are the costs of rushing to the lethal injection table? Execution is a bell that cannot be un-rung.

Beyond the potential for false positives stands the recent consensus published in the *Journal of Criminal Law and Criminology* that "the death penalty does not add any significant deterrent effect above that of long-term imprisonment."[258] Findings by the National Academy of Sciences agreed.[259] Statistics get tossed around on both sides of this argument, but at the very least, there is enough reasonable doubt to give us pause. Human lives are at stake, and as Amnesty International has noted, "You can't take it back."

---

257 Amnesty International, "Five Reasons to Abolish the Death Penalty," May 8, 2019
258 Michael L. Radelet and Traci L. Lacock, "Do Executions Lower Homicide Rates?: The Views of Leading Criminologists," Journal of Criminal Law and Criminology, 2009
259 Daniel S. Nagin and John V. Pepper, "Deterrence and the Death Penalty," National Academy of Sciences, 2012

Such concerns do not trouble Ann Coulter.

In 1989 five black and Latino men were accused of brutally raping a jogger in New York City's Central Park. The crime got national attention, and shortly after the assault, Donald Trump took out full-page advertisements in four New York City newspapers bearing the all-caps demand to "BRING BACK THE DEATH PENALTY. BRING BACK OUR POLICE!" Note his conflation of government-sanctioned executions and law enforcement, which is telling. Trump gleefully admitted that he hated all murderers: "I am not looking to psychoanalyze or understand them. I am looking to punish them."[260]

Understanding what happened in the case of the Central Park Five proved important, however, as another man, serial rapist Matias Reyes, ultimately confessed to the crime in 2001, his confession corroborated by DNA evidence. The five wrongly convicted men, whose original confessions had been coerced, were released, and they subsequently sued the city. Their story was featured in the 2019 Netflix film, *When They See Us*.

In 2019, from his position as President, Donald Trump remained unapologetic and defiant, convinced of the men's guilt, evidence be damned. Echoing his troubling statement about "good people on both sides" after the deadly 2017 white supremacist rally in Charlottesville, Virginia, Trump addressed the Central Park reversal: "You have people on both sides of that."

Cue Ann Coulter and her July 25, 2018, column, "Central Park Rapists: Trump Was Right." Coulter lamented that a politically correct horde of social justice warrior liberals was eager to exonerate "youths of color" against the assault of "a privileged white woman." Coulter was—and remains—completely oblivious to the phenomenon of police coercion and false confessions. She also shares Trump's defiance of the evidence: "Punish them."

---

260 Jan Ransom, "Trump Will Not Apologize for Calling for Death Penalty over Central Park Five," The New York Times, June 18, 2019

I think the Trump-Coulter attitude provides some insight into hard-line conservative thinking on crime: strength before consideration. If some unfortunate souls get crushed under the wheels of justice, they are just necessary collateral damage. The important thing is that America is "tough on crime," a notion soapboxed by countless politicians fueling their campaigns with promises of greater public safety. Taking things slow, extracting the data, and considering the moral, emotional, and financial costs equates to weakness and surrender.

Beyond the problems with the system, I am struck by the issue of dehumanization. This is profoundly slippery ground, because many people think that an attempt to understand a killer automatically translates to empathy or sympathy for the killer and a marginalization of the killer's victims. If we focus on a murderer's upbringing, environment, mental capacity, and any other influencing factors, we take the focus away from the precious son, daughter, spouse, friend, or neighbor left rotting in a ditch. We feel like we are rationalizing, deflecting, and excusing, and strong justice demands firm condemnation and swift retribution. A binary world is simpler and, in many ways, easier to navigate. Good guys punish the bad guys. Who cares why they're bad?

Should we be content to embrace Donald Trump's eagerness to reject understanding? Doesn't solving a problem demand that we follow it to its roots? Or are we content to build our halls of justice upon mere indignation? In my conservative youth, indignation was enough. If I may use her name as a verb, I had Ann Coultered my brain.

I'm not saying I wasn't interested in reversing injustice. More accurately, I was uninterested in the driving forces behind harmful behavior. As such, my culture was constantly swatting at symptoms and ignoring the roots. Any attempts to analyze the criminal brain, the damage of childhood abuse, or behavior-molding environmental forces felt like hesitation. Such hesitation was the domain of weak-minded moral relativists who couldn't commit on an easy good/evil question. The solution to crime was to teach biblical morality and use tough, decisive, even lethal force against society's rogue elements.

There is some truth to this second notion. The hostage-taker must be neutralized in the name of public safety, and sometimes law enforcement's best first option is the trigger. But American conservatives seem awfully eager to lean toward good-guy violence, as seen in its thriving gun culture. There is often little reverence or reservation about taking a life as long as the dead guy is a "bad guy." Dead criminals simply mean fewer villains on the planet. *Why* did they become villains? Who cares?

I think we should care, and as we resist the dehumanization of others, we can ensure that we don't breed glib, callous indifference within ourselves. We don't have to shovel away the soil of our own high ground and devolve into an exuberant mob compensating for one grave by dancing on another. We don't have to become killers to defiantly oppose and decisively prosecute killers—not when there are so many flaws in the process.

Our resistance to the death penalty shouldn't be about the murderers. It should be about ourselves. This stance requires that we examine whether we want justice or mere vengeance and that we make a commitment to remain civilized in this often-uncivilized world. It also requires a realization that, in some cases, killers are made, not born, and society must address the precursors to violent behavior.

A 2017 National Institute of Justice study revealed that "child abuse and neglect have been shown to increase the risk of later forms of antisocial behavior, including violence perpetration and crime in adulthood."[261] The study found that, in middle childhood, females more often responded to childhood physical and emotional abuse by exhibiting depression, anxiety, and social withdrawal. Conversely, males were much more likely to externalize behavioral problems with aggressive displays of hostility and delinquency. Researchers at

---

261 National Institute of Justice, "Pathways Between Child Maltreatment and Adult Criminal Involvement," October 11, 2017

Duke University published their finding that "individuals who had been physically abused in the first five years of life were at greater risk for being arrested as juveniles for violent, nonviolent, and status offenses."[262] The study showed a clear correlation between child maltreatment and subsequent violent behavior, with many children developing "biased patterns of processing social information," more often assigning hostile intent to the outside world and more likely to respond aggressively. These antisocial behaviors are often compounded in those with social and psychological problems. Adults who spent their formative years in an abused, confused, anxious, and fearful state can experience a distorted perception of reality and broken moral cognition.

A few extreme cases of this type of criminal are serial killers Richard Ramirez, Henry Lee Lucas, Donald Gaskins, and John Wayne Gacy, all of whom were horribly abused as children. Aileen Wuornos was abandoned by her mother and raped by her grandfather. Ed Gein was raised in isolation and indoctrinated to be terrified of the evil world outside. Another intriguing case is mob hitman Richard Kuklinski, known as The Iceman. Kuklinski was analyzed on-camera by renowned psychiatrist Dr. Park Dietz in the 2003 HBO documentary *The Iceman and the Psychiatrist*. Dietz revealed that Kuklinski was born with a "genetic predisposition to fearlessness" that might have resulted in prosocial behaviors had it not been for the loveless home life and intense abuse that Kuklinski endured as a child. An abusive or unstable childhood is a common denominator for a great many killers, rapists, abusers, and perpetrators of violent crime.

As unpopular as the notion may be, targeted analysis of murderous behavior shouldn't be considered a betrayal of victims. Sociopaths come in many shades. They are products of nature, nurture, or both. Examining the basis of their behavior isn't a cheat; bypassing the evidence is a cheat. As with scientists who treat cancer while also researching its root causes, we must navigate through our revulsion to

---

262 Jennifer Lansford, et al., "Early Physical Abuse and Later Violent Delinquency: A Prospective Longitudinal Study," Child Maltreatment, August 2007

---

reverse-engineer the crimes and the killers and understand that the solutions to punishing murderers won't fit on an NRA bumper sticker.

With this critical information, society can do more than merely treat the symptoms of violent crime, and we can dial in to the precursors that often mold the monsters among us. Advocacy for abused and potentially abused children seems a good place to start, as we work to safely remove children from the abusive homes that science shows can develop murderous criminals.

Let me close this chapter with some good news. The FBI has recently reported that violent crime, including murders, continues a decades-long overall decline in the United States.[263] The Pew Research Center revealed new data confirming that violent crime has fallen sharply in America over the past quarter century.[264] There are certainly spikes in a few cities, such as Washington and Philadelphia,[265] but the big picture is encouraging: the U.S. is experiencing fewer violent crimes.

Despite the facts, the American public still wrongly believes that the country has become a more dangerous place in the last decade,[266] rooting its perception in emotion over the data. President Trump has been quick to capitalize on those fears. In December 2019 Trump's Justice Department asked the Supreme Court to allow the resumption of executions by the federal government.[267] At the time of this writing, it is still unclear if the court will take up the case. Trump's rallying cry from 1989 continues: "Bring back the death penalty!" (And let's not bother with the pursuit of understanding.)

It's time to reject this rejection of understanding. It's time to commit

---

263 "2018 Crime in the United States," 1999—2018, Federal Bureau of Investigation, Criminal Justice Information Services Division
264 John Gramlich, "5 Facts about Crime in the U.S.," Pew Research Center Fact Tank, October 17, 2019
265 Timothy Williams, "Murder Rate Drops Across U.S., but Not in All Large Cities," The New York Times, September 30, 2019
266 John Gramlich, "Voters' Perceptions of Crime Continue to Conflict with Reality," Pew Research Center Fact Tank, November 16, 2016
267 Sarah N. Lynch, "Trump Administration Asks Top court to Allow it to Resume Federal Executions," Reuters, December 2, 2019

to being informed dispensers of justice. While we should remain strong and vigilant, we must also remain educated and enlightened, countering life's inhumanities without surrendering to them. We can identify the threats to life and limb, remove them from society, and, if necessary, throw away the key. Our prison systems present a host of headaches all their own, but they still present a more civilized, cheaper, less burdensome, and less potentially calamitous solution to America's murder problem.

Ann Coulter may squeal with delight at the torture and execution of another, but I stand with Vicki Schieber. If Vicki can see past her unspeakable grief to help evolve society's notions of justice, you and I certainly can.

CHAPTER TEN:

The Bible Tells Me So: The Reality behind Christianity's "Good Book"

IT WAS DECEMBER 2015. Muslim YouTube hosts Sacha Harland and Alexander Spoor conducted a social experiment for their channel, Dit is Normaal, taking their cameras and microphones onto the streets of the Netherlands to document public opinions. Brandishing a book that was obviously the Qur'an, Harland and Spoor read various verses aloud and asked random people, "What do you think?"

The verses they quoted were sobering, as follows:

> *If you reject my commands and abhor my laws, you will eat the flesh of your own sons and the flesh of your own daughters.*[268]

> *I do not allow for a woman to teach…*[269]

> *You will have to cut off her hand. Do not forgive her.*[270]

> *If two men sleep with each other, they will both have to be killed.*[271]

---

268 Leviticus 26:29
269 1 Timothy 2:12
270 Deuteronomy 25:12
271 Leviticus 20:13

The jarred responders were aghast. "This sounds ridiculous." "How could anyone believe in this? That's unbelievable to me!" "If you've been raised with this book and these kinds of thoughts, it's going to influence the way you think." "To me this sounds like they [Muslims] want to oppress you and force you to believe what they believe." "It bothers me that some people see these old writings as the absolute truth."

Harland and Spoor then asked their interviewees about the Bible versus the Qur'an. The responses were hugely deferential to Christianity. "I think the Qur'an is more aggressive." "The Bible is a lot less harsh and a bit more peaceful." "I think the Bible mostly has a lot of positive things in it."

Of course, you're already ahead of me. Those terrible verses weren't actually from the Qur'an. Harland and Spoor had fitted a Bible with a false cover and quoted Christian scriptures to unsuspecting Dutch ears. The respondents couldn't believe they'd been duped, exclaiming, "Seriously?" "What the fuck?" "You really got me."

Granted, the hosts of *Dit is Normaal* were mostly interested in countering anti-Muslim bigotry in the wake of the November 13, 2015, ISIS attacks in Paris, teaching non-Muslims to recognize their own hypocrisy and prejudice. But the larger lesson applies to Christians worldwide: Believers don't know their own Bible.

Comedian Ron Pearson, a Christian, demonstrated this lack of knowledge further with a 2007 YouTube video[272] recorded at Shepherd of the Hills Church in Los Angeles. Ron asked his fellow churchgoers to name all the Ten Commandments for a prize of fifty dollars. The blank stares he received were both funny and terrifying. Several people couldn't manage even a single commandment. A gray-haired woman finally said, "Thou shalt have no other graven image before thee, or whatever." Another person quoted an incorrect verse from the New Testament. A newlywed was able to quickly rattle off the

---

272 titled "Ron Pearson's 10 Commandment$,"

commandment about adultery. A young woman listed "Thou shalt not kill" and "Thou shalt not commit murder," which are the same rule in Exodus 20:13. Several people responded, "Oh my God!" breaking commandment number three. Only a few were able to rattle off the full ten. Actually, there are two different sets of commandments in the Old Testament, but that's an issue for another book.

Pearson's experiment wasn't a scientific study, but it did effectively provide a window into the mind of America's cultural Christians. These believers talked the talk. They showed up for sermons. They wore the cross necklaces and prayed before meals. But they operated largely in the dark when it came to the essential tenets of their One True Faith.

The Bible is the foundational book for more than two billion protestants and Catholics worldwide. It explains the origins of the universe, establishes a code of behavioral conduct, provides a general timeline for God's Greatest Hits, and contains critical instructions for the afterlife. Ask even the most moderate, most uninformed Christian, "What is the most important book ever written?" and the answer is a reflex: The Bible.

LifeWay Research published a 2017 study revealing that 87 percent of American households own a Bible. The average household has three.[273] Barna lists the Bible as the planet's most-read book, with more than five billion copies sold.[274] Most of the respondents of that study claimed that the Bible "contains everything a person needs to know in order to live a meaningful life." Two-thirds believed that it is the actual word of God.

Fundamentalist Christian organizations agree. The Southern Baptist Convention is the largest protestant denomination in the United States.[275] In its statement of basic beliefs, the SBC declares the following:

---

273 LifeWay Research "Americans Are Fond of the Bible, Don't Actually Read It" April 25, 2017
274 Barna Research "The Bible in America: 6-Year Trends" June 15, 2016
275 Pew Research Center "7 Facts about Southern Baptists" June 7, 2019

The Holy Bible was written by men divinely inspired and is God's revelation of Himself to man. It is a perfect treasure of divine instruction. It has God for its author, salvation for its end, and truth, without any mixture of error, for its matter. Therefore, all Scripture is totally true and trustworthy. It reveals the principles by which God judges us, and therefore is, and will remain to the end of the world, the true center of Christian union, and the supreme standard by which all human conduct, creeds, and religious opinions should be tried. All Scripture is a testimony to Christ, who is Himself the focus of divine revelation.[276]

The second largest protestant group in the U.S., the United Methodists, is slightly less strict, yet it still proclaims the Bible an "inspired" and "sacred" book, canonized under God's authority and "vital to our faith and life."[277]

The Assemblies of God's "Sixteen Fundamental Truths" declares the Bible "verbally inspired of God" and "the infallible, authoritative rule of faith and conduct."[278]

Fundamental Christianity is clear. The Bible is the most important book—ever. Yet it's usually little more than a paperweight. Christian obliviousness is so rampant, publications such as *Christianity Today* have produced action plans to reverse "The Epidemic of Bible Illiteracy in our Churches."[279] The 50 percent of Americans who read some form of scripture[280] often do so not with an analytical eye, but instead dial into the uplifting, motivational verses of personal affirmation and divine purpose, verses like:

"For I know the plans I have for you," declares the LORD, "plans to

---

276 Southern Baptist Convention "Basic Beliefs" sbc.net/aboutus/basicbeliefs
277 United Methodist Member's Handbook
278 General Council of the Assemblies of God "Our 16 Fundamental Truths"
279 Christianity Today/The Exchange "The Epidemic of Bible Illiteracy in our Churches" Ed Stetzer July 6, 2015
280 Center for the Study of Religion and American Culture "The Bible in American Life" December 2017

---

prosper you and not to harm you, plans to give you hope and a future." —Jeremiah 29:11

"Delight yourself in the LORD, and he will give you the desires of your heart." —Psalm 37:4

"And we know that in all things God works for the good of those who love him, who have been called according to his purpose." —Romans 8:28

"Therefore, if anyone is in Christ, he is a new creation; the old has gone, the new has come!" —2 Corinthians 5:17

"See what great love the Father has lavished on us, that we should be called children of God!" —1 John 3:1

Christians further dial into pleasantries with supplemental Bible study guides, books so popular that retailers feature them in designated sections. The Red Letter Bible uses red ink to specifically highlight the words of Jesus Christ, the great New Testament teacher who commanded his children to seek first the Kingdom, let their light shine before others, ask and receive, be vigilant, love enemies, and do good works. This is Cherry Picking 101, a cafeteria plan for truth, and it plays like a sweet symphony to the Fox News crowd.

Ainsley Earhardt hosts a Fox Nation broadcast called *Ainsely's Bible Study*, which frames happy scriptures against the feel-good personal stories of American celebrities. It's a feast of empty calories for the Christian masses, strumming heartstrings and reinforcing emotional justifications for belief. Ainsely hosts *Fox & Friends* with her evangelicalism front and center. Why is a news network promoting Christianity? She's a known face at megachurches and the Christian Broadcasting Network. In an Easter interview with Fox News host Steve Hilton, Ainsley promoted her 2018 book, *The Light Within Me* and lamented un-Christian ideas that threatened to "destroy the fabric of America."[281] On that same program, Fox host Mike Huckabee pitched a "Judeo-Christian ethic" as "the tuning fork of our culture."

These conversations took place on a *news* network and were propagandized by hosts, not guests. They're proclamations of Christian nationalism. Ainsley and Huckabee are in good company.

- *Fox & Friends* cohost Steve Doocy spun the 2015 mass church shooting in Charleston, South Carolina, as an attack on the Christian religion.[282] In fact, the shooting was racially motivated.

- On her radio show, Fox News host Laura Ingraham pitched her Christian opposition to same-sex marriage by comparing it to incest.[283] Interestingly, Ingraham's gay brother told the *Daily Beast*, "I think she's a monster."[284]

- Fox host Tucker Carlson promoted David Horowitz's 2019 book, *Dark Agenda: The War to Destroy Christian America* with the blurb, "Read this disturbing but vital book." On *Fox & Friends*, Carlson recently lamented that "educated people" perpetuate "Christianphobia."[285]

- On the Fox News broadcast *Justice*, Judge Jeanine Pirro criticized Barack Obama's order that U.S. intelligence agencies investigate Russian interference in the 2016 presidential election. She sided against America's FBI in favor of Russian dictator Vladimir Putin, partially on religious grounds. In her words, Putin is "at least a Christian."[286] Perhaps the murderous Putin was getting moral guidance from the Old Testament.

- On November 21, 2019, *Fox Business* host Lou Dobbs praised President Donald Trump for appointing judges who uphold

281 Fox News "The Next Revolution with Steve Hilton" April 1, 2018
282 Fox & Friends June 17, 2015
283 The Laura Ingraham Show April 29, 2015
284 Daily Beast "Laura Ingraham's Brother Goes to War Against Her" September 12, 2018
285 Fox & Friends February 1, 2015
286 Fox News Justice with judge Jeanine Pirro, opening statement December 11, 2016

Christian values with the word "hallelujah." This is a business show?

- Fox News prime time powerhouse Sean Hannity executive-produced and appeared in the 2017 Christian drama film *Let There Be Light,* starring Kevin Sorbo. The movie depicts a hardened atheist who converts to Christianity after an auto accident. Hannity and Dallas mega-pastor Robert Jeffress often exchange appearances on each other's platforms, their holy bromance wrapped in Christian nationalism. Sean Hannity has long defended the Christian god with deistic arguments invoking "energy" that cannot materialize "out of nothing."

- On May 13, 2007, in a spirited face-off against atheist author Christopher Hitchens, Hitch offered the observation to Hannity: "You give me the awful impression—I hate to say it—of someone who hasn't read any of the arguments against your position ever."[287]

The late and greatly missed Hitchens had tapped into a root problem with American Christianity: a high percentage of believers 1) know little about their own Bible, and 2) have rarely—if ever—been meaningfully challenged. When presented with queries about the Bible's origin or congruity, or when shown the uglier shades of Yahweh or Jesus peppered throughout scripture, cultural Christians are often nonplussed. They also—almost always—remain rigid and steadfast, content to be both unswayed and uninformed while simultaneously professing the historical, scientific, and moral truth of a book they do not understand.

I once thought I knew my Bible. My Christian school classes gave tests on scripture memory verses and held Bible drills, contests where students quickly flipped to specific verses on command. I fared well in these competitions. I had a fair grasp of the Old Testament's greatest hits: creation, Adam and Eve, the fall, the flood, the Ten Commandments, Moses and pharaoh, David and Goliath, Elijah

---

287 Hannity's America May 13, 2007

and the fiery chariot, Samson, Jonah and the fish, and so on. New Testament studies were much more common, with constant focus on the birth, life, teachings, death, and resurrection of Christ. I was taught basic concepts about the End Times, but beyond the showing of dramatized rapture films such as *A Thief in the Night*, my school focused little on the Book of Revelation. Mine had been a "skip to the good parts" exercise in Bible instruction, and I wore my blinders well into adulthood.

In my 2012 autobiography, *Deconverted: a Journey from Religion to Reason*, I described the time in my life when my own doubts finally prompted me to examine the Bible with a more objective and critical eye. The chapter titled "The Edge of the Sword" contains a long list of Old Testament atrocities I'd never before seen or acknowledged: Lot offering his own daughters to be raped by a crazed mob (Genesis 19:6-8). Yahweh instructing Moses's army to execute all Midianite woman and children except for the virgins kept as the spoils of war (Numbers 31:17-18). Instructions for beating slaves (Exodus 21:20-21). The death sentence for rape victims who didn't adequately cry for help (Deuteronomy 22:23-24). God threatening rape as punishment for rebellion (2 Samuel 12:11-12) and forcing victims to marry their rapists (Deuteronomy 22:28-29). The execution of a man for picking up twigs on a Saturday (Numbers 15:32-36). The stoning of children for disobedience (Deuteronomy 21:18-21). God commanding infanticide (Joshua 6:21), accepting human sacrifice (Judges 11:29-39), and endorsing the slaughter of half a million people (2 Chronicles 13:27).

My skeptical journey through the New Testament was a gentler ride, but I was still confronted by hugely troubling verses where Christ threatened to turn families against each other (Matthew 10:35) and cast unbelievers into "everlasting fire prepared for the devil and his angels" (Matthew 25:41).

Those examples are but a toe in the bloody ocean, but they rattled my bones. Had Sacha Harland and Alexander Spoor tried their Qur'an/

Bible experiment on me, I would have likely failed like the others.

I'd also been trained to take a linear view of scripture, one verse at a time, one book at a time. I had never cross-compared the stories to see the many, many contradictions. The book that fundamental Christianity called "totally true and trustworthy" was a conflicting mess. Genesis had two contradicting timelines for Creation. The Bible lists three different people as the father-in-law of Moses, the man who brought two conflicting versions of the Ten Commandments down from Mount Sinai in Exodus and Leviticus. The Ark of the Covenant was constructed by different people in different Old Testament books. The gospel of Luke's account of Satan tempting Jesus reverses the order of events from the fourth chapter of Matthew. The nativity story disagreed from gospel to gospel on the appearance of the angel, the census, Herod's decree, the manger, the virgin birth, the wise men. Matthew and Mark had different timelines for Jesus's cursing of the fig tree. Christ carried his own cross in John 19 but was helped by Simon in the other gospels. The New Testament said that Judas both hanged himself and had his bowels burst upon a field. Matthew, Luke, and John had conflicting accounts of Jesus's last words on the cross. The Bible had four contradictory versions of Jesus's empty tomb. These examples, and so many more, exist in black and white for anyone who dares to look.

Finally, there was the bizarre stuff that made no sense: God's refusal to allow temple access to any man with crushed testicles (Deuteronomy 23:1). David giving King Saul a wedding dowry of two hundred Philistine foreskins (Samuel 18:25-27). Jesus conjuring tax money out of the mouth of a fish (Matthew 17:24-26). Ezekiel being commanded by God to lie on his left side for 390 days while cooking his food over a fire made of human feces (Ezekiel 1:1-16). Yahweh declaring shrimp an abomination (Leviticus 11:10). Balaam having an argument with his donkey in Hebrew (Numbers 22:28-29).

The book of Matthew describes the following astounding event that took place just after Christ's death on the cross:

At that moment [when Jesus gave up his spirit] the curtain of the temple was torn in two from top to bottom. The earth shook, the rocks split, and the tombs broke open. The bodies of many holy people who had died were raised to life. They came out of the tombs after Jesus's resurrection and went into the holy city and appeared to many people. —Matthew 27:51-53

The dead became undead and walked the streets of Jerusalem, yet no contemporary historian—not one—felt compelled to chronicle this jaw-dropping supernatural occurrence. For validation of this story, one is left with only the book of Matthew, which was not actually penned by Matthew, and which scholars estimate was written between 80 and 90 CE, decades after the alleged zombie parade.

Beyond these wild Bible stories lay the question of authorship. When Genesis 1:1 describes a pre-Adam earth that was "formless and empty," who was reporting this event, and from where? From what vantage could the author of Genesis see the light separated from darkness, the vault separating the waters, the conjuring of land and the animals, and the creation of Adam and Eve?

Apologists like to explain that *tradition* credits Moses as the author of Genesis. In other words, "We think it's Moses." What absolute and perfect truth rests on the admission "We think?" And how could Moses report events that took place before his own birth? Beyond the impossibility of a firsthand account lies the implication that God "divinely inspired" the words of Genesis into Moses's ears. This apologetic is even more alarming: *We think it was a guy named Moses... who was hearing voices.*

Imagine this scenario. You're the father of several children, and you return home to discover that your house is on fire. In the flaming second-floor windows, you can see the terrified faces of your small children. You can feel their panic. You can hear their screams for help. Because you designed the house, you're aware of a special shortcut past the danger, a shortcut that would effectively save your children's lives. Yet instead of rushing up to the house and giving the instructions firsthand, you shout the information to a third party. You then watch in silence as that person recites—from memory—the information to a another person. That person passes the message to yet another person who disagrees with its interpretation and changes the message before passing it on again. Continue this scenario several hundred more times, until—finally—someone rushes back to the house and relays the escape route. For the duration of this incident, you stand quietly near the back of the street.

This is what theologians expect us to believe about the Bible. With Heaven and Hell in the balance, God sent his critical salvation message via history's longest game of Telephone.

Acts chapter 9 tells the story of Saul on the Damascus Road. As he plotted to murder Jesus's disciples, Saul was suddenly blasted with white light from Heaven. He collapsed to his knees, and Jesus spoke to him directly, commanding him to repent and directing him toward Damascus. This encounter transformed Saul's life, and he subsequently became Paul the Apostle, alleged author of no fewer than thirteen New Testament books.

Why would Saul receive clear instructions firsthand while history's billions are left with a contradictory book subjectively translated into conflicting versions, in thousands of languages, by a humanity so pathetic and misguided that it screwed up everything else in the world? And even if Jesus presented a Bible to us personally, would he choose the King James Version? The New American Standard? The Scofield Study Bible? The Revised Standard Version? The New English Translation? The Living Bible? Would he require the early Greek and Hebrew versions, two languages that almost seven billion people don't speak or understand?

Here's an important point. *No living Christian has ever read the Bible.* They've read only a copy of a copy of a copy of a translation of an interpretation of a copy, ad nauseum, of the Bible. No original manuscripts exist, and no historian has been effectively able to verify any of the Bible's authors. Even the Gospels were penned long decades after the alleged life and death of Christ. Mention this problem to contemporary Christians, and you'll likely hear an argument from popularity, "The Bible is the most printed book in history. Of course it's true!"

Is popularity a worthy measure for truth? Isn't mass delusion still delusion?

Christianity, like all fundamentalist religions, is also quick to embrace its own magic while rejecting the supernatural stories within other faiths. Present the Islamic claim that Allah conjured the earth out of smoke in six days (Qur'an 41:11), and the Christian will scoff. "Yahweh created the world from nothing." Declare that the first man was formed from a single clot of blood (Sura 96:12), and the Christian will chuckle with disdain. "Adam was created out of dirt." Pronounce that the prophet Muhammad rode into the heavens on the back of a winged beast (Qur'an 17), and the Christian will cringe in disbelief. Jesus levitated to Heaven after his dead body was reanimated."

Despite Islam's global popularity as an Abrahamic religion, its magical claims are rejected while Christianity's magical claims are embraced. Skepticism for one myth. Acceptance for the other.

Bestselling author A. J. Jacobs conducted a wildly entertaining experiment that he chronicled in his 2008 book, *The Year of Living Biblically: One Man's Humble Quest to Follow the Bible as Literally as Possible.* Jacobs decided to spend twelve months obeying literal tenets of the Bible. Scripture prohibited mixed fabrics, so Jacobs obsessed over clothing labels and even examined fibers under a microscope to ensure purity. Leviticus forbade the trimming of beards, so Jacobs let his facial hair grow. He wore sandals and carried a walking stick. He bought a ram's horn and blew it at the start of every month. He refused to touch his wife during her period, as she was "unclean."

He relied on volunteers to open the refrigerator on the Sabbath. He built a sukkah hut in his living room. He covered suggestive magazine photos with masking tape. He refused to eat shellfish.

In one humorous exchange with a seventy-five-year old man who admitted being an adulterer, Jacobs attempted to stone him with tiny yard pebbles. The stranger stomped off in disgust.

A. J. Jacobs is a self-professed secular Jew, and his Year of Living Biblically resulted in no profound spiritual revelation, although he admitted to enjoying the habit of prayer. Mostly his experiment revealed how bizarre and dangerous a literally lived Christianity would be. Jacobs constantly had to bend the rules just to keep himself and others safe from calamity. I'm reminded of this popular Internet meme:

So why do Americans cling to their Bibles with such fervor? I don't think their allegiance is about the Bible as much as a larger attraction to religion itself. The Bible is a totem which can be read, skimmed, or ignored, but the religion it represents is embraced without question, and there are many reasons that religion has survived and thrived throughout human history.

Tribalism

In the infancy of our species, humans sometimes benefited from religious thinking. Psychiatrist Dr. Andy Thomson has explored how religions served to create tribal bonds between non-kin.[288] Tribes were stronger than the individual. Tribes encouraged cooperation. Tribes were more effective at warding off threats. On the African savannah, primitive tribes assuaged their own significant ignorance on the big questions about birth, life, purpose, and death. Religions provided an opportunity for tribes to expand beyond small groups into larger, safer, stronger families forged by beliefs. In the times when humans perceived a flat earth, feared deadly predators, and got swallowed up in natural disasters they couldn't explain, religions provided mechanisms for coping and survival.

Pattern Seeking

Humans have evolved as pattern seekers. Our ancestors once used pattern-seeking to ensure survival. As psychologists and brain scientists have long observed, our brains have long been dot-connecting machines that constantly see patterns, even when none exist. In our ancient past this tendency was beneficial for survival. The rustling of a tree branch implied a predator in the brush, even if it was only the wind, but the false positive was a safety net that ensured that you would live another day. In a phenomenon known as apophenia, people are constantly sensing patterns: butterflies in Rorschach ink blots, animal bodies in cloud formations, a human face on the surface of Mars, hidden messages in radio frequency white noise, UFOs in starry skies, the linking of coincidental life events, even conspiracy theories about 9/11 or the moon landing. We see complexity. We see groups and clusters. We see recognizable imagery. And our brains usually interpret these things as patterned—designed—elements.

---

288 Why We Believe in God(s): A Concise Guide to the Science of Faith Dr. Andy Thomson 2011

Platforming religious notions of design are apologists such as Dr. William Lane Craig and Dr. Stephen Meyer, who claim that the universe is finely tuned by an intelligent designer. For them, patterns are everywhere, the gears proving the existence of a watchmaker. Through their bullhorns about design, these apologists often wax about complexity. Complicated mechanisms imply the expert touch of an engineer whose handiwork is revealed in things such as the human eye, the feathered bird wing, interlocking bones, and the genome. Of course, these apologists are completely uninterested in examples of poor design: blind creatures with eyes, deaf creatures with ears, pelvises in legless animals, vestigial organs, degenerating eyesight, parasites that eat their living hosts, the loss of 50 percent of fertilized human female eggs, redundant DNA, deadly earthquakes and hurricanes, a sun that gives us cancer, and the extinction of 99 percent of all animals that have ever lived.[289]

(Note: Despite their embrace of Christianity, these apologists are making claims that are remarkably deistic, promoting a faceless prime mover instead of an involved and personal god. This jump from deism to theism requires a huge leap of faith.)

Programming

In 2008 Richard Dawkins wrote, "A child is not a Christian child, not a Muslim child, but a child of Christian parents or a child of Muslim parents."[290] Indeed, children are born relatively blank slates in terms of religion, yet even a cursory look at religious families reveals the phenomenon of inherited belief. (Roughly eight in ten people raised by Protestants still adhere to Protestantism.[291] This trend is also reflected in the Muslim religion, and to a lesser degree, Catholicism.)

Are the Muslim parents of Yemen producing Southern Baptist children?

---

289 The Biology of Rarity: Causes and Consequences of Rare—Common Differences W. E. Kunin, Kevin Gaston 1996
290 The God Delusion Richard Dawkins 2007
291 Pew Research Center "1. Links Between Childhood Religious Upbringing and Current Religious Identity" October 26, 2016

Are the Hindu parents of India producing Mormon children? Are the Christian parents of the United States producing Muslim children? Of course not. In most cases, the faith of one echoes into the other. Family and geography remain the major determining factors for someone's religious convictions.

Young children are little trust machines that rely completely on their guardians to survive. The same parents/caregivers who supply food, shelter, and protection also engage in a hand-me-down distribution of ideas—sometimes bad ones. To ensure the reproduction of their religions, parents often isolate their children in private religious schools or engage them constantly in religious rituals. Tragically, these children are often sequestered from anyone and anything deemed different, and they're trained to accept only in-group ideas during their most impressionable years, a period that Christian children's ministries often refer to as "the four-to-fourteen window."

A popular Internet meme.

Tell a twenty-five-year-old that donkeys talked, humans lived to be nine hundred years old, and a virgin was impregnated by a ghost, and he'll laugh you out of the room. Tell a trusting six-year-old the same thing, and you'll likely get earnest acceptance. I gave a 2013 speech titled "Get Them While They're Young," describing many of the tactics Christianity uses to brand itself onto the brains of vulnerable children.[292]

Ignorance and Fear

In the Information Age, we can no longer rest on the excuse of ignorance, yet many religious people—like their ancestors—engage in religious thinking as a coping mechanism, an emotional crutch, and too often, an opportunity for intellectual laziness sustained by fear. Fear of being wrong. Fear of uncertainty. Fear of death. Fear of eternal torment. This phenomenon explains the popularity of Pascal's Wager, the assertion that "I'd rather claim God and be wrong, because belief costs nothing, while nonbelief risks Hell." This wager is a fallacy. It pretends that a life of misdirected belief wouldn't be wasted.

In his 2007 book *Breaking the Spell*, philosopher Dr. Daniel Dennett writes about "belief in belief" and common responses by the faithful when challenged.

> If anybody ever raises questions or objections about our religion that you cannot answer, that person is almost certainly Satan. In fact, the more reasonable the person is, *the more eager to engage you in open-minded and congenial discussion, the more sure you can be that you're talking to Satan in disguise! Turn away! Do not listen! It's a trap!*[293]

This thought-stopping attitude has effectively shielded religions for thousands of years, reinforced by Christian claims that doubting is a sin or a Satanic attack and Hell awaits the unbelievers. Jesus Christ himself declared to the disciple Thomas that "the one who doubts is like a wave of the sea, blown and tossed by the wind. That person should not expect to receive anything from the LORD."[294]

---

292 FreeOK 2013 "Get Them While They're Young" by Seth Andrews (on YouTube)
293 Breaking the Spell: Religion as a Natural Phenomenon, Daniel C. Dennett, 2008
294 James 1:6-7

The faithful often compensate for any hidden doubts with outward projections of confidence, and as Dr. Dennett observed, the mere act of claiming a belief fortifies resolve. Bible verses reinforce this with constant commands to believe: *Believe* in the Lord Jesus, and you will be saved. You *believe* in God; believe also in me. Repent and *believe* the good news! If you declare with your mouth, "Jesus is Lord," and *believe* in your heart that God raised him from the dead, you will be saved.

Notice how the Bible encourages belief, not knowledge. Christians are expected to accept the biblical party line on faith. Hebrews 11:1 says, "Now faith is confidence in what we hope for and assurance about what we do not see." Under the microscope this verse makes no logical sense. We're supposed to have confidence in something based on what we hope, not the confirmation of what is, and we're supposed to be sure about something that we cannot see or verify.

This is belief in belief.

Welcome to the spoon-fed intellectual infancy of millions of American Christians who have embraced notions of religious superiority and national destiny without question. They lay claim upon the Constitution, but they do not know it. They speak a Christian language, but they do not understand it. They listen to the sermon, but they do not dissect it. They brandish the Bible, but they do not read it. They condemn science, even as they rely on it. And in their isolation chambers, from their church pews, on their talk radio shows, in their study guides, and through their Fox News champions, they receive 24/7 affirmation that Christianity is true because they believe it, and they believe it because it's true.

Control

When I was a devout Christian, I firmly believed that the Bible was a book about freedom. Only later did I recognize its death grip upon almost every aspect of my life. Christianity declared that I had been born broken and required repair. Christianity determined my friends and activities. It framed my education. It intruded into my dating life and lurked in my bedroom. It informed my political opinions and voting habits. It bled my bank account. It fueled my career choice. It was a constant and proactive autocrat, using terms like "commandments" to narrow my options.

Throughout history, the powerful have utilized religion. How many dictators and kings tightened their holds on the masses with the invocations of God? How many of the privileged have used religion to justify their consolidation of power? How often have theocrats felt emboldened to tell others how to live? The state-church of the Roman Empire once used its military to quell dissent and mandate public worship. The Christians of the Medieval Inquisition tortured non-adherents on the breaking wheel. The Catholic Church once persecuted and convicted scientists such as Galileo for contradicting its dogma. Today's Islamist nations demand daily prayers to the east, the veiling of women, even the execution of apostates. American Christian nationalists stake a legal and moral claim to pretty much everything of value in their country. God is their golden ticket. As the ancient Roman philosopher Lucius Annaeus Seneca famously wrote, "Religion is regarded by the common people as true, by the wise as false, and by the rulers as useful."

Refocusing on the issue of American Christian nationalism, we must remember that all of this—the whole of Christian influence—is propped upon an anonymously written book filled with conjuring, spells, blood magic, slavery, torture, human sacrifice, infanticide, genocide, and the tale of a superbaby born to save billions from the failing of God's Perfect Plan. And while there's likely some utility in embracing the more humanistic attributes of some religions (community, common goals, charity), there's no excuse for shutting down our reasoning centers in matters of truth. If there's no good reason to believe a claim, there's no good reason to accept, protect, or promote that claim. If this means raising a critical hand to the dubious notions of our ancestors, reading more than one book, summoning our courage, and challenging authority, so be it.

It's the twenty-first century. It's time for humanity to do better. Let us read our Bibles with objectivity, curiosity, skepticism, criticism, and the desire not simply to believe, but—whenever possible—to know for sure.

CHAPTER ELEVEN:

Abortion: Science, the Soul, and the Question of Personhood

IT WAS JULY 1992. Governor Bill Clinton was on the presidential campaign trail. His limousine was about to transport him from New York's InterContinental Hotel to Central Park for his morning jog when he was approached by a man asking for an autograph. The man—Christian broadcaster Harley David—suddenly tried to hand Clinton a clear plastic container. Inside the container was a fetus.

Harley David was best known as sidekick to Christian talk host and radical anti-abortion activist Randall Terry. The two men had orchestrated the stunt to be broadcast nationally on the syndicated radio show *Randall Terry Live*. Bill Clinton quickly retreated into his limousine, and Harley David was arrested.[295] Randall Terry's broadcast was carried on an affiliate of the station where I worked, and I heard the scenario as it played out in real time.

Bill Clinton and Randall Terry represented two opposite sides of the abortion issue. Bill Clinton had long expressed a personal opposition to abortion, but he supported Roe v. Wade, the landmark 1973 Supreme Court decision that protected abortion rights under the Constitution. (Clinton is an example of someone who might oppose abortion personally yet respects the law and female reproductive

---

295 The New York Times "Protestor Thrusts Fetus at a Surprised Clinton" July 15, 1992

autonomy.) Randall Terry had founded the radical anti-abortion organization Operation Rescue and been arrested more than forty times for blocking entrances to abortion centers and protesting on private property. He ran for the U.S. House of Representatives in 1998 under the Right to Life Party, and he pathetically tried to challenge Barack Obama in the presidential primaries of 2012. Terry's single focus was the morality and legality of abortion. He opposed birth control pills as a "human pesticide"[296] and demanded jail time for all women who get abortions.

The New York stunt with the fetus was ostensibly supposed to humanize the abortion issue and force Bill Clinton to confront his endorsement of "child murder." Clinton minimized the encounter as "no big deal," but that exchange revealed much about anti-abortion attitudes and the desperation of evangelicals to stop the practice. Randall Terry's tactics were considered extreme by most mainstream Christians, but they—and I—shared his opinion that "It's a child, not a choice." Life was a miracle that began at conception, the sperm and egg marrying in divine destiny, immediately producing a tiny human soul that would soon express itself beyond the womb and find its place in eternity.

This is a perspective that many pro-choice activists miss. I attended the 2012 Imagine No Religion 2 conference in British Columbia, and a panel of abortion activists spoke at length about the evangelical assault on female reproductive rights and the patriarchal edicts of Christian fundamentalism. They were rightly concerned over Christianity's attempts to procreate itself into dominance, patriarchal notions of female subjection, and religious control over humankind. Yet none of the panelists focused on a key and driving force behind Christianity's opposition to abortion: the sincere desire to protect human life. The panelists were striking the target, but they had missed a ring. If choice advocates genuinely seek to change minds and the culture, conversations with the opposition must be rooted in understanding—perhaps even (gasp!) empathy—for the often sincere and good

---

296 As quoted on MTV's True Life in April 2013

intentions that drive the war on reproductive choice. As Cassandra Clare once said, "No one is ever the villain of their own story," and choice advocates will help themselves by focusing their energies less on shouts and accusations and more on dialogue and education. We should, whenever possible, foster communication instead of mere clamor. I wasn't insulted out of my religious beliefs, and I'm not convinced we can insult anti-choice activists out of their convictions. Theirs is an insular world in desperate need of a larger perspective, a perspective that you and I can provide.

In my radio days, conservative attitudes about abortion were constantly reflected in the songs of Contemporary Christian Music. Singer Kathy Troccoli portrayed a child in heaven asking God to forgive its mother for having an abortion.[297] Christian metal band Barren Cross pleaded with America to "stop the killing" and described torn bodies of babies in garbage bags.[298] Guitarist Phil Keaggy produced the 1995 song "The Survivor," sung from the perspective of a baby born alive after an abortion. Even the secular group Creed, a Christian radio darling, lamented that "only in America we kill the unborn to make ends meet."[299] Today, from the broadcast dial to the bookstore to the pulpit to the dinner table, Christianity echoes this lament, and many activists are absolutely sincere when their T-shirts and bumper stickers say Pro-Life. For them the fight against abortion is an effort to defend a human being not yet able to defend itself.

If pro-choice activists do not understand this mindset, they will have tremendous difficulty overcoming it. I know it's unpopular to suggest that we develop empathy with our ideological opponents, but empathy is critical for awareness, and we must acknowledge that many anti-abortion activists are genuinely good, kind, compassionate, and moral people who exist far from the radicalism of Randall Terry. They're not trying to demean or diminish women. They're not focused on dominance or control. They're simply motivated to prevent what

---

297 Kathy Trocdoli "A Baby's Prayer" 1997
298 Barren Cross "Killers of the Unborn" 1988
299 Creed "In America" 1997

they believe is the murder of a child. From this vantage, we can see that many anti-abortion activists are desperately fighting for what they think is a moral position. They're trying to do the right thing. Carl Sagan says in his article titled "The Question of Abortion: A Search for Answers:"

> Of the many actual points of view, it is widely held--especially in the media, which rarely have the time or the inclination to make fine distinctions--that there are only two: "pro-choice" and "pro-life." This is what the two principal warring camps like to call themselves, and that's what we'll call them here. In the simplest characterization, a pro-choicer would hold that the decision to abort a pregnancy is to be made only by the woman; the state has no right to interfere. And a pro-lifer would hold that, from the moment of conception, the embryo or fetus is alive; that this life imposes on us a moral obligation to preserve it; and that abortion is tantamount to murder. Both names--pro-choice and pro-life--were picked with an eye toward influencing those whose minds are not yet made up: Few people wish to be counted either as being against freedom of choice or as opposed to life. Indeed, freedom and life are two of our most cherished values, and here they seem to be in fundamental conflict.[300]

I've met some pro-choice influencers who would read the above paragraph and feel betrayed. How could any advocate for a woman's bodily autonomy even imply that abortion opponents might be morally motivated people? Those evangelicals are anti-woman. They're anti-choice. They're anti-human rights! And with these protestations, the indignant remain locked on the effects instead of a root cause: the desire to protect a defenseless soul.

I can hear the protestations of many. *Why is a man rendering an opinion on the abortion question? Who cares what he thinks? He's a man.*

---

300 "The Question of Abortion: A Search for Answers" by Carl Sagan and Ann Druyan (excerpted from chapter 15 of Sagan's 1997 book Billions and Billions: Thoughts on Life and Death at the Brink of the Millennium)

I reject these kinds of purity tests regarding human rights issues. I don't need to be black to grasp that racism is immoral and why. I don't have to be ex-Muslim to see the moral contradictions in Islam. I can be straight and promote LGBT rights. I can be non-military and oppose unjust wars. And I can be male and value gender equality and reproductive autonomy, engaging in moral reasoning alongside my fellow human beings. These are human-rights issues, on the table for discussion across the board, especially recognizing that the abortion issue is often decided by couples, not just an individual. With the critical question of personhood in play, rationalists across tribal lines should do what rationalists do: approach the issue respectfully to achieve the most rational and ethical answer. My small contribution here is, I hope, a perspective on many anti-choice activists who are not motivated by a desire to subjugate women but genuinely grieve over their perceptions of child murder.

I understand that the often-noble intentions of the faithful produce some genuinely horrifying results, and the United States has seen recent examples of fearful, ignorant, and sometimes bigoted God warriors exerting biblically justified control over individual reproductive choices. A prime example is Alabama's 2019 Human Life Protection Act, a near-total ban on abortion, even in cases of rape and incest, which was passed in the Alabama Senate by twenty-five white men. Other states such as Georgia, Ohio, Kentucky, Mississippi, and Louisiana have banned abortion after six weeks, before many women even realize that they're pregnant. In 2019 an unprecedented surge in Republican-majority states passed anti-abortion laws, those paths ultimately leading toward an imminent Supreme Court challenge of Roe v. Wade.

Beyond the legislation lay the consequences to those denied access to safe abortion. Dr. Diana Foster, director of research at the University of California San Francisco, helmed The Turnaway Study, the largest study to examine unwanted pregnancy and abortion in the United States.[301] A survey of about one thousand women revealed serious

---

301 Ansirh.org/research/turnaway-study

consequences for denying abortion and requiring women to bring an unwanted pregnancy to term, including the following:

- Health complications such as eclampsia and even death

- A greater likelihood to stay with abusive partners

- Anxiety, depression, and suicidal thoughts

- Financial distress and inability to meet basic family necessities

According to the survey, most women who sought abortion after twenty weeks "were delayed because they did not realize they were pregnant." About half of abortion patients were using contraception.[302] Women denied an abortion had almost four times greater odds of a household income below the federal poverty level and three times greater odds of being unemployed. Beyond socio-economic and emotional challenges, fetal birth defects remain a serious issue. Planned Parenthood highlights many anecdotes along this line, including the story of Christie B. of Virginia, who had actually planned her pregnancy but discovered that her daughter would be born with congenital diaphragmatic hernia. She said, "My husband and I were confronted with two equally horrible options—carry the pregnancy to term and watch our baby girl suffocate to death upon birth or end the pregnancy early and say goodbye to our much-wanted and much-loved baby girl." Christie terminated the pregnancy at twenty-one weeks, an action that is currently illegal in seventeen states.

Regardless of whether the anti-abortionists' motivations are noble or disgraceful, it's clear that the future of reproductive choice is on the bubble. Mainstream Christians make no distinction between a human being, a person, and a soul. The fertilized egg is a human. The developing embryo is a human. The newborn infant is a human. Much like the idea of the Holy Trinity—Father, Son, and Holy Spirit—these forms are both unique and identical, and they bear a divine fingerprint.

---

302 Guttmacher Institute "Induced Abortion in the United States" 2017

For a moment, let's come back to the notion of the soul. Ask an everyday Christian to define the soul, and you'll likely get some nebulous response about an unseen energy that exists within the human heart and mind. This soul can't be detected by medical instruments, so it can't be measured or quantified. It's a lifeforce that transcends the physical world and constitutes our core self, passing from this earthly plane into another realm after death. Christianity declares that the soul resides within a temporary physical shell, and it is uniquely human. While other species in the animal kingdom may have eyes and ears, fingers and toes, a heart and lungs, blood and bone, they do not—they cannot—possess a soul. A human soul carries with it the important attributes of identity and, at least initially, it is inherently good, as demonstrated by common accusations against terrible people: "They have no soul."

Variations on the soul have long been reflected throughout philosophy and religions, yet they exist beyond any hard interpretation or scientific experiment. Soul claims are not demonstrable and remain supposedly, conveniently unfalsifiable. In 2017 I interviewed Dr. Julien Musolino, neuroscientist and professor of cognitive psychology and psycholinguistics at Rutgers University. Dr. Musolino wrote the 2015 book *The Soul Fallacy: What Science Shows We Gain from Letting Go of our Soul Beliefs*. A survey of his university students revealed three common notions about the soul, as follows:

1) It's immaterial and non-physical. Separate from the body.

2) It's "psychologically potent," driving consciousness, free will, personality, emotion, and decision-making.

3) It's immortal.

In his book Dr. Musolino rightly notes that these concepts of an immaterial, immeasurable soul make no sense, because "the soul hypothesis is also a claim about biology" and can be investigated scientifically. When believers fondly like to say, "As the spirit moves you," they reveal the key problem: a motivating spiritual force should and would have an observable effect on the physical brain/body. Science would be able to detect the influence of the soul as it generates thoughts, ideas, emotions, and actions within the machine of the mind. Yet no soul has ever been observed, and every "eyewitness" claim about an otherworldly plane fails the burden of proof and can be otherwise explained by brain chemistry, deception, or self-deception. It's a claim without evidence, a phantom without form, a popular notion that flounders upon the most rudimentary investigation. No matter how many apologist rationalizations litter the shelves of religious bookstores, the soul operates exactly as it would if it didn't exist. There's simply no good reason to believe in it.

Still, approximately 80 percent of U.S. citizens embrace some type of heaven,[303] a place where the soul resides after physical death. Given that significant number and the fact that 167 million Americans claim some flavor of Christianity, it becomes easier to understand why nearly half of the population opposes abortion.[304] Often, that opposition isn't motivated by a desire to discriminate against or control women but is instead laser focused on the unborn child, the precious soul, the human life that has no ability to defend itself. That rallying cry stirs the righteous to battle. Defenseless children are under attack, so God's army must mobilize. Ultimately, this is an evangelical crusade to defend a soul residing among the multiplying cells.

That position was certainly mine when I was a young evangelical. I wasn't opposed to contraception, but once fertilization took place, the die was cast, and termination of the pregnancy was murder. The irony was that, by that standard, Yahweh was the most prolific abortion doctor in human history.

Sex education isn't exactly a strong suit in the Bible Belt, but even a cursory look at the human reproductive process reveals that 50 percent of all fertilized eggs wash out during menstruation. Total prenatal

---

303 Pew Research "Most Americans Believe in Heaven...and Hell" November 10, 2015
304 Gallup "Pro-Choice or Pro-Life: 2018-2019 Demographic Tables" Values and Belief Polls

losses approach 70 percent in the first weeks after fertilization.[305] Sexual intercourse actually produces more dead fertilized eggs than live babies. As believers in an Intelligent Designer, American Christians are left to explain why each of those soul-bearing eggs is excreted into the sewers. Psychologist Dr. Valerie Tarico noted the following:

> A lot more eggs and sperm get made than will ever hook up with each other. Many more eggs get fertilized than will ever implant. And more zygotes implant than will ever grow into babies. The world's major religions, including even the most extremist forms of Christianity, Islam and Judaism, tacitly acknowledge that these reproductive false starts are not people by declining to name or baptize the ones that women's bodies expel on a regular basis.[306]

She's correct. Even the more educated Christians aren't rushing to daily baptize hundreds of thousands of failed embryos. Dr. Tarico referenced the famous Duggar family, stars of the reality television show, "19 Kids and Counting." Declaring contraception a sin, Jim Bob and Michelle Duggar parented nine girls and ten boys, proudly proclaiming that they had left the procreation process to God. Tarico rightly notes that based on the live births Michelle Duggar delivered, she also "flushed somewhere between seventeen and seventy-five embryos in order to get the family they have." Yet this case produces no righteous indignation by the anti-abortion crowd, and I suspect two reasons.

1) Christians believe that the God who creates life also has the right to end it. *The Lord giveth, and the Lord taketh away.* His reasons aren't important, and whatever those reasons, it's likely that earthly mortals couldn't comprehend them, anyway. "Who has known the mind of the Lord? Or who has been his counselor?" (Romans 11:34)

---

305 U.S. National Library of Medicine, National Institutes of Health, "Early Embryo Mortality in Natural Human Reproduction: What the Data Say" June 7, 2017
306 "Who Aborts the Most Fertilized Eggs? Families Like the Duggars" Dr. Valerie Tarico, January 9, 2015

2) Abortion opponents engage only when female choice is involved. A woman has decided to derail God's sovereign life-and-death determination, and driven by hubris, selfishness, or desperation, she has placed her own life in priority over a "child." Whether the interventionists see women as biblically subject to male authority, or whether the focus is solely on protecting the embryo, the result is control: control of sexual behavior, of reproductive choices, of the female gender. Anti-abortion activists—often men—ostensibly speak for God as they lay claim upon the uterus in the name of "life," and that crusade preempts all other considerations, even bodily autonomy and personal boundaries.

Once we discard notions about the magical spark of divinity and root the abortion issue in the real world, how do human rights advocates address the complex issue of *personhood*, especially regarding a fetus developed into the second and third trimesters? Beyond the overarching reality that a woman's body is her own, and with the central question of personhood in play, I think this is a subject that people, both men and women, should be able to discuss, and our discussion starts with the fertilized egg. A single cell becomes two cells and begins to multiply further. Around day ten the fertilized egg has relocated from the fallopian tube and implanted itself in the lining of the uterus, where some cells become the placenta and others become the embryo. At four weeks that embryo is the size of a poppy seed.

"Fetal-heartbeat bills" falsely declare that a "viable" person exists at the sixth week of gestation, when fetal cardiac activity can be detected. In reality it's merely a rudimentary cluster of pulsing cells, something gynecologist and columnist Jennifer Gunter more accurately terms "fetal pole cardiac activity."[307]

---

307 Drjengunter.com "Dear Press, Stop Calling Them 'Heartbeat Bills" and Call Them 'Fetal Pole Cardiac Activity' Bills" December 11, 2016

Human embryo at six weeks
image: Vincent Deporter

Dr. Michael Gazzaniga is a professor of psychology at the University of California, Santa Barbara. He remains one of the world's leading researchers in cognitive neuroscience, and in chapter one of his 2006 book *The Ethical Brain*, he describes the human embryo in its early stages:

> Even though the fetus is now developing areas that will become specific sections of the brain, not until the end of week five and into week six (usually around forty to forty-three days) does the first electrical brain activity begin to occur. This activity, however, is not coherent activity of the kind that underlies human consciousness, or even the coherent activity seen in a shrimp's nervous system. Just as neural activity is present in clinically brain-dead patients, early neural activity consists of unorganized neuron firing of a primitive kind. Neuronal activity by itself does not represent integrated behavior.[308]

In other words, these early electrical firings are unarranged signals happening weeks before the cerebrum starts to develop, and more than a month before the frontal and temporal lobes of the brain become apparent. As described by Dr. Gazzaniga, at week thirteen, "the fetus is not a sentient, self-aware organism at this point: it is

308 The Ethical Brain: The Science of our Moral Dilemmas by Michael S. Gazzaniga 2006

more like a sea slug, a writhing, reflex-bound hunk of sensory-motor processes that does not respond to anything in a directed, purposeful way." The nervous system doesn't become cohesive until roughly the seventeenth week.

Statistically two-thirds of abortions occur by the eighth week of pregnancy, and 88 percent occur within the first twelve weeks.[309] The canard that these early abortions kill tiny babies with fingers and toes is popular among evangelicals, but the indignant are actually referring to a barely developed cluster of cells, and when pressed, many abortion opponents can't differentiate between a human embryo and the embryo of a puppy, dolphin, or cow.

Like the human sperm and unfertilized egg that came before, a human embryo might be in the strictest sense "alive," but it is not a person. If anti-abortion activists believe that a cluster of developing cells constitutes human life, they must then be asked to defend the hundreds of millions of wriggling sperm cells produced in ejaculation and all unfertilized eggs expelled from the female body every month. After all, sperm and egg represent genetic halves of potential human beings. (I once heard a salient question for the Intelligent Design crowd: "If your birth is a matter of divine destiny, why did God bother with the millions of other sperm?")

Of course, religious institutions such as the Catholic Church do lay claim upon these genetic halves, forbidding contraception beyond the "rhythm method" linked to a woman's infertile period during the menstrual cycle. The church has long been an instrument of sexual control, especially over women, and has proven consistently and tragically late to the science and human rights party. This is true for America's major protestant religions, as well as other faiths worldwide. Ironically, 68 percent of Catholic women ignore the priests and use some form of "highly effective" contraception, whether sterilization, IUD, or the Pill.[310]

---

309 Guttmacher Institute "Induced Abortion in the United States"
310 Guttmacher Institute "Religion and Family Planning Tables"

Skipping forward to the tenth week of human pregnancy, the face of the fetus begins to take on human features. In the second trimester, fingers and toes become developed and defined, and the fetus has eyelashes, fingernails, and even hair. The nervous system is beginning to function, and the six-inch-long form has genitalia and a discernable heartbeat. At six months, the bronchioles of the lungs begin to develop. By week thirty-two, the fetal brain can control breathing and body temperature.

For many the development of distinctly human features heightens the sense of moral dilemma, with the ill-defined "viability" of the fetus triggering passionate debate between—and sometimes within—the opposing camps. Over 90 percent of abortions are performed in the first trimester, 7 .6 percent of all abortions are performed between the fourteenth and twentieth week, and 1.3 percent are performed at twenty-one weeks or later.[311] So when does an unviable fetus become a human person, and does a living organism have rights that supersede the privacy and bodily autonomy of its host?

Anti-abortion opponents have long seized upon late-term horror stories, an example being President Trump in his 2019 State of the Union address: "New York cheered with delight upon the passage of legislation that would allow a baby to be ripped from the mother's womb moments before birth." Trump egregiously misrepresented New York law, which allows abortions after twenty-four weeks if "there is an absence of fetal viability or the abortion is necessary to protect the patient's life or health." Trump also declared that the governor of Virginia had "stated he would execute a baby after birth."[312] In fact, Governor Ralph Northam was speaking about non-viable fetuses born with severe deformities being assessed and resuscitated if the mother and family desired it.

This kind of fearmongering is effective among evangelical conservatives. Their indignation is often not rooted in the laws and the data, but instead knee-jerks into panic over sermons about babies tossed

---

311 Centers for Disease Control and Prevention "CDCs Abortion Surveillance System FAQs" 2016
312 New York Reproductive Health Act, signed into law January 9, 2019

into dumpsters in the name of liberal selfishness and convenience. Many declare that no maternal condition would ever warrant a third trimester abortion, a claim that simply isn't true. The American College of Obstetricians and Gynecologists explained that women in late pregnancy might experience "premature rupture of membranes and infection, preeclampsia, placental abruption, and placenta accrete" that might endanger their lives. In those cases, doctors choose to terminate the pregnancy rather than lose the pregnant woman to blood loss, stroke, or septic shock.[313]

Drifting from an emphasis on early-pregnancy privacy toward later-pregnancy viability, Roe v. Wade provides unrestricted abortion rights in the first trimester and tightens the conditions as time progresses. The Supreme Court also gave individual states permission to determine their own boundaries in the later stages of fetal gestation, and states' laws reflect the political slant and religiosity of their citizens. Some states require a licensed physician; others do not. Some states restrict insurance coverage of abortion; others do not. Some states have a mandatory waiting period and required counseling; others do not. Alabama, Louisiana, Mississippi, Ohio, Georgia, Kentucky, and Arkansas are among the most restrictive states, while New York, Vermont, Maine, California, Washington, and New Mexico are among the states providing greater protections on abortion rights.

As an Oklahoma evangelical I was once radar-focused on the rights of the unborn yet largely ambivalent about babies outside the womb. Once an umbilical cord was cut, my indignation waned. In retrospect I realize that I wasn't "pro-life" as much as I was "pro-birth." I've met very few evangelicals who would ever consider adopting a baby "rescued" from abortion. The baby might be sentenced to a miserable existence, but at least it was existing outside the womb. Somehow this fact is supposed to constitute an argument for the sanctity of life.

I, along with an alarming number of pro-lifers, conveniently ignored

---

313 Washington Post "Tough Questions—and Answers—on 'Late-Term' Abortions, the Law and the Women who Get Them." February 6, 2019

---

issues such as the availability of contraception, societal restraints, economic hardships, education, partner challenges, and unreadiness for parenting. I'd bought the lie that women almost always spent their post-abortion lives wallowing in shame, sadness, and regret. (Most have no regrets.[314]) I had reduced the rights of women against the greater rights of an unborn "soul," and I tethered my opinions to a religion long guilty of subjugating women for being women. Our moral outrage was sincere, but it was also myopic and discriminatory. Even as we expressed verbal sympathy for those with unwanted pregnancies, my family and my church painted abortion rights advocates as rudderless, godless baby killers, our hypocrisy at full volume as we empathized with a cluster of cells while ignoring or vilifying those who decided not to develop them to term.

As Donald Trump has recently added two conservative activist judges to the Supreme Court, Roe v. Wade is again a target for evangelicals, yet that law remains a reasonable approach to the complex problems of bodily autonomy, female reproductive choice, fetus viability, and personhood. As we discuss the ethics of terminating pregnancy at late-term, we better our perspectives by understanding how fetuses develop, when those fetuses might survive outside the womb, and ultimately, by acknowledging that a woman's body isn't the property of any other person, any church, or any government. States like Alabama might declare themselves the arbiters of personal decisions, but they're rationalizing greater health risks, greater misery, and an unjustifiable invasion of privacy.

At this point we should discuss the elephant in the room: patriarchy. The opposition to abortion carries a strong element of male dominance, female subjugation, and sexual shaming. Throughout history, overtly and subconsciously, men have demanded submission from females. A great example is this popular chart revealing Christianity's God-ordained hierarchy, with men accountable to God, and women accountable to men.

---

314 New Scientist "Majority of Women Who Have an Abortion Don't Regret It Five Years On" January 13, 2020

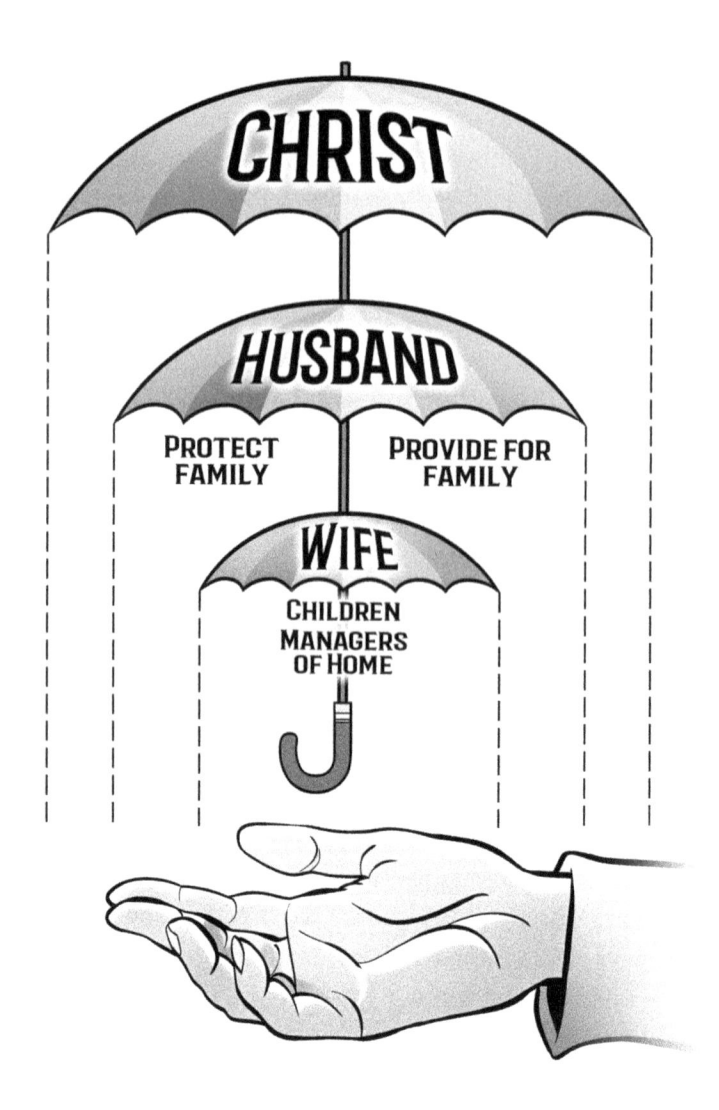

Christianity has evolved many of its notions about the woman/wife as homemaker and child-bearer, but the Bible remains clear in its attitudes about females.

- In the Garden of Eden, God punished Eve's disobedience through the pain of childbirth. "I will greatly multiply thy sorrow and thy conception; in sorrow thou shalt bring forth children." (Genesis 3:16)

- In the same verse, Eve's sexual desire was part of a divine curse, because she had tempted Adam with the forbidden fruit. "And thy desire shall be to thy husband, and he shall rule over thee." At the beginning of the world, Yahweh (a male) and Adam (a male) had already staked a claim to a woman's identity, sexuality, and reproductive processes.

- Still drawing from the curse, scripture mutes the voices of females. "Let the women learn in silence with all subjection. But I suffer not a woman to teach, nor to usurp authority over the man, but to be in silence. For Adam was first formed, then Eve. And Adam was not deceived, but the woman being deceived was in the transgression." (1 Timothy 2:11-14)

The Bible constantly treats females as secondary, even disposable. Throughout scripture, women were tossed to mobs of rapists,[315] stoned for being rape victims,[316] sold into slavery,[317] barred from God's temple,[318] banished during menstruation,[319] burned as witches,[320] forced to miscarry "illegitimate" fetuses,[321] kidnapped as war plunder,[322] and generally shamed as temptresses.[323] As Eve brought Adam into sin, the woman brought humankind into sin and calamity, and females have remained targets of shame and blame ever since, forever locked under the divine edict to submit, submit, submit.[324]

Given their second-class status, it's interesting to watch so many Christian women embrace their assigned roles. I distinctly remember a conversation with a friend—a Christian mother of three—who felt quite content to stand in her husband's shadow. She eagerly admitted that she left the big decisions to the man, and she was adamantly anti-abortion on moral grounds. (I don't know her position on

---

315 Genesis 19:1-8
316 Deuteronomy 22:23-24
317 Exodus 21:7-11
318 Exodus 38:8
319 Leviticus 12:4-7
320 Exodus 22:18
321 Numbers 5:13-31
322 Numbers 31:16-35
323 Proverbs 7:9-27
324 Colossians 3:18

contraception.) Her example combines two common elements: subjugation to male authority and a fervent conviction that an embryo has a soul. Both attitudes are rooted in Christianity and informed by a long and sordid history of misogyny and sexual control.

I wasn't conscious of feeling any sense of ownership over women when I was a devout Christian. My mother was—and is—a strong woman in an equal partnership with my father. She rejects most of the Bible's anti-woman verses. Mom was a fierce opponent of abortion on the very grounds first discussed in this chapter: the defense of the unborn soul. I inherited this conviction, and my anti-choice opinions targeted the fetus with little focus on the womb in which it developed. The *result* of my attitudes was anti-woman discrimination, but the *motivation* itself was not, and I'm convinced that this common catalyst must be acknowledged by pro-choice activists seeking cultural change.

This requires some stretching on our part, and that stretch is difficult. Empathy often feels like acquiescence, the opposition seems ideologically unreachable, and we resign ourselves to steamrolling over our adversaries with sheer verve. We don't think we can talk them down, so we shout them down, and opportunities for discourse devolve into trench warfare where both sides dig into established positions. Certainly there are necessary moments for raised voices and strong demonstrations, but we can balance those against genuine opportunities to listen to, empathize with, and educate the victims of bad ideas.

I was once a victim of indoctrination and ignorance, yet my attitudes evolved, not because I was provoked and humiliated, but because rationalists saw me in three dimensions and took time to show me the better path. I was free to discard magical souls taught by a bigoted Bible, and I found my place along human rights activists spanning genders, colors, and cultures to defend and celebrate reproductive choice. I'm a living example that this transformation is possible, and if it is possible for me, it's certainly possible for others as well.

CHAPTER TWELVE:

The Gay Agenda:
Biblical Bigotry and the
Myth of the Traditional Family

IT WAS SOMETIME in 1998, I think. I was an adult of thirty, and I was telling an associate about an upcoming road trip. She began the conversation, and I responded. It went as follows:

"You going to be around this weekend?"

"No. I'm driving down to Dallas."

"Dallas?"

"Yeah. I'm going to go visit Corey."

[pause]

"You're staying there?"

"Yes."

"At his house?"

"Yes. He's got a guest room."

[pause]

"At his house?"

To my associate it didn't matter which room I'd be sleeping in. I was going to stay in the house of a gay person. I could see her contempt at the very notion.

Corey was my best friend. We'd met in high school and connected immediately, sharing common and usually geeky interests such as sci-fi and horror films. Corey was a year older and stood six inches taller at six feet, seven inches, but we were buddies. We had that special gift of close friends: to be able to do something—or nothing—without ever feeling bored or fidgety. We were both storytellers and loved to write. We had Sting's "Nothing Like the Sun" album constantly playing. We frequently quoted *Star Trek*, the original series and *Next Generation*. We loved Toho Godzilla films. And tacos. And Tolkien. And a thousand other things. Corey was—and is—my brother.

In the high school and college years, he and I had often stayed at each other's homes. A decade later my fundamentalists friends grimaced at the thought. Homosexuality was so perverse, so abominable, they didn't even want to be in its proximity. Had Corey walked into their living room, they would have smiled politely, but only politely, not with enthusiasm, warmth, and affection. Those things might be mistaken for tolerance. Tolerance might be perceived as acceptance. And God condemned homosexuals.

Only a few years earlier, I had felt the same.

Corey had kept his sexuality such a secret that no one ever suspected, including me. I can only imagine his struggles around Christian parents, in a Baptist school, in red state Oklahoma, in the largely phobic 1980s. Whatever was happening with his thoughts and feelings, he buried it deep. He spoke about females. He dated females. He married a female. When that marriage ultimately failed, I simply chalked it up to another divorce statistic. After all, Christians have the same divorce rate as the rest of the country. Sometimes things just don't work out. *C'est la vie.*

It was 1996. I was well into my career as a Christian radio host and still devoutly religious. Corey had moved to Dallas five years earlier, and we often kept in touch through the mail. His latest letter arrived, and I gently pulled the typed pages from the envelope. Instead of the buoyant tone present in our usual banter, though, this letter read more like a quiet proclamation, which it was. At some point, far from my field of view, Corey had decided to be honest with himself, and after much consideration, he decided to be honest with me. The line on the second page said, "I am gay."

What he should have said is, "I am gay, but it's none of your goddamn business." Fortunately for me, Corey has a generous heart.

In the twenty-first century, Christian culture has relaxed a bit regarding homosexuals. Of course the major denominations—Baptists, Assemblies of God, United Methodists, Roman Catholics—preach hardline anti-gay sermons, but churches largely don't panic like they once did. They're measured. Calmer. More strategic. Many churches open their doors to homosexuals for the purpose of luring them into "gay conversion therapy," abominable, Bible-based "re-education" programs designed to "cure" them of unnatural desires. A few religious groups welcome gays without judgment, and churches like the Episcopal Church and the United Church of Christ even allow the ordination of LGBT clergy.

In the 1990s, this was not the case. The United States was still reeling from the AIDS crisis, and somehow even sexless infections through blood transfusions and dirty needles were often declared the fault of homosexual perversion. Evangelical America was disgusted with gays. Gays brought sin. Sin brought calamity. Calamity brought God's judgment. In 2001, Reverend Jerry Falwell and CBN host Pat Robertson would even blame America's acceptance of gays for the attacks of 9/11.[325]

The Bible was crystal clear on homosexuality. It was a heinous perversion that warranted execution.

> If a man has sexual relations with a man as one does with a
> woman, both of them have done what it detestable. They are

---

325 The 700 Club September 13, 2001

to be put to death; their blood will be on their own heads."
—Leviticus 20:13

Christian apologists disagree on the Bible's death sentence for gays. Many will mutter something about Jesus's New Covenant, which cancels Old Testament Law. (Does this negate the Ten Commandments as well?) A few will insist that the Bible never mandated a literal death penalty but instead was speaking of a spiritual death in the hereafter. A few extremist Christian preachers continue to embrace capital punishment for gays, a recent example being Pastor Grayson Fritts of All Scripture Baptist Church in Tennessee. Fritts preached a May 2019 sermon declaring that LGBT people were freaks worthy of death, ultimately begging the government to send a riot team to a June 22 Pride parade for arrests, trials, and executions.[326] (Note: Pastor Grayson Fritts is a police detective at the Knox County Sherriff's Office. A member of Tennessee law enforcement supports the killing of homosexuals. Let that sink in.)

Perhaps most interesting to me are the Christians who have somehow, against the text of their own Bibles, decided that God loves and accepts gay people. The website **gaychurch.org** fawns about "God's love" and directs users to "an affirming church." In 2020, the United Methodist Church proposed splitting the denomination in half so that one side might support same-sex marriage and LGBT clergy. Author Matthew Vines published the book *God and the Gay Christian: The Biblical Case in Support of Same-Sex Relationships.* There's even a pro-LGBT revision of the classic KJV scriptures called *The Queen James Bible.* All of the anti-gay verses have been sliced out or altered.

Don't misunderstand. I'm all for religious enlightenment. A moderate church beats a dogmatic one hands down, and I appreciate the widening tent of nonjudgmental faiths. As Bob Dylan famously sang, the times they are a-changin'. It's a step in the right direction, but no

---

326 New York Times "Tennessee Pastor Who Is Also a Detective Calls for LGBT People to Be Executed" June 15, 2019

amount of moderation changes the foundational Bible that props up the Christian religion.

Twenty-five years ago, the LGBT community was experiencing what the Civil Rights Movement had experienced in the 1960s. The American mind was starting to expand, but many corporations, institutions, and "straight" people had dug in their heels, often on religious grounds. Much of the gay world remained closeted or ostracized. A Pride parade in the 1990s was often more demonstration than celebration, with pleas for policy changes at the Centers for Disease Control (CDC), challenges to the Catholic Church's restrictions on LGBT people, and demands for more AIDS funding. A common Pride T-shirt read, "We are all living with AIDS."

I was terrified that Corey would one day live with AIDS. My narrow, indoctrinated brain overloaded at the mental picture of Corey the Gay. Leaning into my Bible, I grieved at the dangers, the perversion, the waste. I conjured wild images of bathhouse debauchery, saddened at how far my brother had fallen. I flipped through a mental Rolodex of slurs, not even realizing I used them as slurs: fag, sissy, fairy, queer. Corey had become one of them. He was the Other. After ten years of fast friendship, he was no longer a brother. Corey had become a label.

I waited several days to respond to Corey's letter, my reply laced with judgment. I wasn't cruel or hateful. Mostly I was scared. This previously hidden part of Corey's identity frightened me. In my letter I said something about fearing for his safety, and I rattled off some pious paragraphs about disappointment. I may have even quoted a scripture. I signed my name and popped the letter in the mailbox.

We didn't speak for a year.

After those twelve months I realized how much I had been struggling with his absence. There was a gaping hole in my life. I had blown off a cherished relationship. I had cheated myself of a loyal friend. My platitudes about "godly sexuality" were hollow and unsatisfying, and even though I still believed that homosexuality was a sinful "choice," I also realized that my life had been better with Corey in it. I cleared my head, steeled my resolve, and broke the silence. I wrote another letter, an olive branch that I hoped he might return to me. Corey wasted no time in responding. He was kind. He was understanding. He was forgiving. And we began to mend what had been broken.

I didn't emerge from Christianity until 2007, but I look back at those days and wonder if my steps toward Corey were also my first steps out of fundamentalism. In order to see a friend in three dimensions, I had to do something previously unthinkable; I had to reject parts of my own Bible. Homosexual acts are an abomination?[327] *That seems harsh.* Gays are Sodomites deserving of punishment?[328] *Corey is a better man than most Christians I know.* LGBT people deserve death?[329] *That's just wrong.*

The cherry-picking began. I'd long skipped past the inconvenient parts of the Bible, but this was the first time I did so with real purpose. This is a common story among apostates. They don't emerge from the coma instantly, but instead wake up slowly. Their eyes adjust to the light. They sluggishly move atrophied muscles. They become strong enough to sit and then to stand. To walk and then to run. The journey can be an arduous one.

I discarded the specific anti-gay verses in God's Perfect Word. I was— finally—applying a moral standard *to* the Bible from *outside* the Bible. I'd examined God's ethical code and reasoned that either 1) God was wrong or 2) I was wrong, but rebellion and Corey's friendship were worth the cost. My own evolved ethical systems nudged me from bigotry toward acceptance. I was becoming conscious. Later in my life, I'd direct that critical eye toward the rest of Christianity, and I would finally learn to run.

---

327 Leviticus 18:22
328 Deuteronomy 23:17-18
329 Leviticus 10:13

With the benefit of hindsight, I've become acutely aware of how often I had shielded anti-gay bigotry and Christian privilege under the benign-sounding term "traditional family values," a phrase I mention often in this book. It's a noble notion on its surface. "Tradition" conveys stability, honored memories, a respect for the past as it informs the present. "Family" conjures 1950s Americana, the Norman Rockwell painting of a pure and trouble-free nuclear family. "Values" is a declaration of moral superiority, as good Christians value goodness, purity, rightness, and justice.

Just as the privileged have used the phrase "law and order" to silence dissent, Christian nationalists have used the phrase "traditional family values" to press their specific religious agenda. It's a rigged game, as anyone watching from the cheap seats would see a challenge to "traditional family values" as a defense of depravity. *Who could oppose tradition, family, and values?*

Note the name chosen by the anti-LGBT, fundamentalist activist and lobbying group, the *Family* Research Council, originally founded in 1981 by evangelical James Dobson's organization, Focus on the *Family*. FRC lobbies for its version of "family values" by campaigning against same-sex marriage and LGBT people serving in the military, and it has linked homosexuality to pedophilia. The Family Research Council's views on gays, linked to a "biblical worldview,"[330] is so toxic that the organization is listed as a hate group by the Southern Poverty Law Center.

Right-wing media often speaks nobly of "family values." Senator Marco Rubio spoke at Catholic University of America to "support traditional marriage."[331] In 2012, when former president Barack Obama expressed his support for same-sex marriage, four-time divorcee Rush Limbaugh blasted Obama's "war on traditional marriage."[332] Two years later Limbaugh ranted that CBS's hiring of Stephen Colbert as Late Show host was part of the liberal conspiracy, "an assault on

---

330 frc.org/about-frc
331 The Catholic University of America" Washington DC July 23, 2014
332 Rush Limbaugh radio show May 9, 2012

traditional American values, conservative values."[333] Conservative host Glenn Beck, a Mormon, has lamented how "the traditional family unit" has been devastated by "secularism and liberal policies."[334] Beck is on the roster, along with Donald Trump, Dana Loesch, Oliver North, Dennis Prager, and others, for the 2020 Values Voter Summit, a conference that attracts a yearly audience of more than three thousand under the theme of preserving "the bedrock values of traditional marriage, religious liberty, sanctity of life, and limited government that make our nation strong."[335]

And of course, Fox News's most influential hosts agree.

- In 2013, *GQ* magazine published an interview with *Duck Dynasty* star Phil Robertson, who—using the Bible—compared homosexuality to bestiality. He also claimed that black farmers were "singing and happy" before the "pre-entitlement, pre-welfare" Civil Rights era. Phil's comments were vile enough to result in his suspension from his show, yet Fox News's Sean Hannity rushed to Robertson's defense, protesting that Robertson was merely presenting "old fashioned traditional Christian sentiment and values."[336]

- Fox News's Judge Jeanine Pirro was featured speaker at the 2018 Guardian of the Family Banquet. The event organizers proudly declared that they wanted to "unleash biblical citizenship on New Jersey." Pirro leapt into hot water in March 2019 when she suggested that practicing Muslim Representative Illhan Omar's wearing of the hijab might mean she was "antithetical to the United States Constitution." The implication, of course, was that true Americans are Christian, not Muslim or any other religion. To its credit, the Fox News network condemned Pirro's statement after public backlash, but it's laughable to think Fox's culture is one of religious inclusion. Ever

333 Rush Limbaugh radio show April 10, 2014
334 Glenn Beck "Serial: Breakdown of the Family"
335 valuesvotersummit.org/about
336 Sean Hannity Show December 18, 2013

seen a Fox News segment about the War on Ramadan? Of course not.

- Fox host Laura Ingraham said in her 2008 book *Power to the People*, "Even for those who reject the idea that God ordained the family in its traditional form, our decades of experimenting with the alternatives should be pretty good evidence that humans, by their unchanging nature, are most happy in the setting of a traditional family."

There is so much wrong with Ingraham's thinking here. First, she sets the premise that a proper family is ordained by (her specific) God. Secondly, she declares that even those rejecting her premise would benefit from it. Next she says that non-heterosexual families are experiments carried out in recent decades (non-hetero relationships are a recent phenomenon?). Finally, she makes the unfounded claim that families with "traditional" hetero parents are happier ones.

- Even the ousted Fox News host Bill O'Reilly published a defense of "traditional values" his 2017 book, *Old School: Life in the Sane Lane*,[337] an embarrassing love letter to a mythical American heyday. Shamelessly invoking the Greatest Generation, O'Reilly divided the United States into past and present, strong and wimpy, stalwart and snowflake, right and wrong. He yearned for a simpler time of square-jawed American nobility, when codes of honor still bound the U.S. together. He even showed a photograph of John Wayne and fawned over the tough-guy patriotism of Navy Seal sniper Chris Kyle, whose memoir *American Sniper* described the act of killing as "a lot of fun." (Chris Kyle's credibility has long been in question. He once falsely boasted that he also shot "looters" during the aftermath of Hurricane Katrina[338] and lost a defamation lawsuit filed by Jesse Ventura after Kyle claimed to have punched Ventura in a bar fight.)

---

337 Old School was co-authored by Bruce Fierstein
338 The New Yorker "In The Crosshairs" by Nicholas Schmidle, May 27, 2013

Throughout his book O'Reilly painted his world in the simple lines of black and white. He even created a parental advice chart with two columns, one labeled "Old School" and the other "Snowflake." He mocked university degrees containing the words "comparative, ethnic, or studies." He painted caricatures of "social justice warriors" offended by Christmas carols, the national anthem, and NASCAR. He idolized Clint Eastwood's famous portrayal of Dirty Harry, a hero who ignored due process and blew the bad guys away. O'Reilly lionized Sean Connery, the famed James Bond actor who once told Barbara Walters it was sometimes appropriate to strike a woman. And Bill grieved America's slide into moral relativism. He seemed unconcerned about the irony of advising his readers about morality and justice in the same year when he and Fox paid six women nearly $50 million to settle various sexual harassment lawsuits.

Bill O'Reilly longs for the era of the man's man, not the "girly man."

The Fox News culture, including right-wing radio, informed many of my former attitudes about the Gay Agenda, a poorly defined threat constantly warned about in conservative circles. I was genuinely fearful that this agenda would arrive on my doorstep and do something. What would it do? I had no idea. But the Gay Agenda was coming! It was coming for our families, our children, our churches, and our government! My pastors referred to the "gay lifestyle." Friends and associates often referred to "fags" and "homos." I was being programmed to fear an encroaching army of homosexuals that wanted to *infect us with gay*!

Ultimately—finally—I discovered what the Gay Agenda was, and it was startlingly, astoundingly, reasonable.

It was equality.

Long-marginalized and often-persecuted LGBT people were merely asking to not be vilified, not be dehumanized, not be locked out of marriage opportunities, not be refused healthcare, not be denied service in public establishments, and not be blamed for everything from child abuse and bestiality to pandemics and terrorism. Non-heterosexuals weren't coming to take over the feast; they were simply wanting a seat at the table. They hadn't come to alter the sexual identities of straight people, but rather, they sought to live in a world where (often religious) heterosexuals couldn't discriminate against them. Equality.

This desire for equality makes sense, even when viewed against the rest of the animal kingdom. Even a cursory observation reveals the commonality of non-heterosexuality throughout nature, with same-sex behavior documented in more than 450 species of animals worldwide.[339] Have the mallard duck, bottlenose dolphin, giraffe, penguin, lion, bonobo, tortoise, and spotted hyena all somehow rebelled against God? Or is it fairer to accept that non-hetero behavior is common and natural across the spectrum of animal life?

It's rather amusing how distressed anti-LGBT people get at the idea of sharing this world. They justify bigotry while standing on the book of Leviticus. They fear God's wrath for abiding the Sodomite. They call same-sex attraction a "lifestyle choice," completely oblivious to their own hard-wired attractions. Parents worry that homosexuals will somehow change the sexual identity of their children, as if hetero parents give birth only to hetero kids, and many seem nervous that the legality of same-sex marriage will cheat or destroy the marriages of everybody else.

My friends, if the notion of gay marriage threatens your relationship, then one of you is gay.

Hardline conservatives seem anguished about a great many agendas out there. The Liberal Agenda spreads heinous ideas like protecting Constitutional state/church separation, establishing public

---

339 Biological Exuberance: Animal Homosexuality and Natural Diversity by Dr. Bruce Bagemihl 2000

healthcare as a right instead of a privilege, creating opportunities for long-marginalized minorities so they might break cycles of poverty, reproductive choice, a free and accountable press, gender equality, race equality, and sexual equality. Regardless of where you fall on the political spectrum, consider which American political party is more clannish and restrictive, and which is more accepting and emancipatory. It's not the Democratic Party that invokes God as a justification to oppose same-sex marriage, deny abortion access to women, prevent new social programs, and claim moral and national superiority in a cloud of xenophobia.

I'm not deifying the Democrats, even though I am one. Politics is messy. Politicians are often messy. And I'll be the first to admit that liberals can be just as tribal as conservatives when examining the best and worst in their own camp. But I'm a liberal for a reason. I didn't choose the label. I simply examined my views on key issues—gay marriage, the role of government, the death penalty, healthcare, state/church separation, immigration—and realized that I aligned much more with the platform of the Democratic Party. Once a die-hard, true-blue, Limbaugh-loving conservative, I came to embrace what I felt were better ideas. I changed my mind. I evolved my thinking. And while the Democratic Party (like every political party in history) will never be immune to corruption, cads, scandals, and misguided ideas, it remains the one major party that locks arms with my best friend and fights for his right to be loved, to be equal, to be an American, to be human. It fights for Corey.

I have no interest in branding my identity onto someone else, and I'm not threatened at all by those who are different from me, who merely want to live and love in peace, who simply want their deserved place at the human table. I reject the lie that elevating another diminishes me, and I hold strongly to the belief that there can be a place on earth for every color in the rainbow.

In that sense, with this richer and more enlightened definition of the term, I suppose it can be said: I'm a supporter of the Gay Agenda.

CHAPTER THIRTEEN:

The Looney Left: Liberals Aren't Immune to Bad Ideas

HERE AT MY final chapter I have little doubt that my non-evangelical conservative readers are frustrated. Frustrated at the religious infection of their own party. Frustrated at the daily headaches caused by Christian nationalists. They support state/church separation. They don't concern themselves with the private choices of others. They don't like Rush Limbaugh or watch Fox News. They despise conservative extremist groups. And they hold to a more fiscal conservatism that supports lower taxes and smaller government on philosophical grounds. Agree or disagree with them, they aren't represented by the theocrats bleeding superstition into a government designed to be secular. Yes, they have a responsibility to stand up and speak out against Christian nationalists in their own house, and many are frustratingly silent, but it's important to see the fiscal conservative in an impartial light. I know a great many right-wing evangelicals, but I also know some non-religious conservatives who don't fit into the God-and-Country cookie cutter.

Republicans are three-dimensional human beings, and they hold their political views for a spectrum of reasons that don't fit on an Occupy Democrats Internet meme. It's important to acknowledge this fact. It's important to be fair.

Along the lines of fairness, I also feel compelled to speak about problems in my own liberal camp. I remain convinced that liberalism remains the humanistic and best position, but I've also seen far-left factions knee-jerk into such extreme "wokeness" that they damage the causes they ostensibly promote. These sects are fiercely tribal, prone to hyperbole, frustratingly simplistic, and are constantly tossing tasty red meat to the Fox News crowd. In their daily discontent, these fringes bring flailing machetes into theaters for delicate surgery, and they sometimes fuel unrest where it shouldn't exist. Their default attitude is constant—even recreational—outrage.

Of course, outrage is a correct response to the genuinely outrageous problems in this world. We should be outraged at the constant state/church violations happening in the United States. We should be outraged at Donald Trump's abuse of presidential power. We should be outraged at the Catholic Church's shielding of rapist priests from criminal prosecution. We should be outraged at forced child marriage in Islamist nations. We should be outraged at the 40,000 Americans who die from gun-related injuries every year. We should be outraged that Scientology oppresses and threatens its cult members. In no way am I declaring that anger isn't justified in the face of corruption, abuse, and tyranny. Anger is the proper response, and it is often a healthy motivator to create positive change.

Yet we've all seen the calls for justice spill into very problematic territory. I'm a strong proponent of social justice programs and efforts toward racial and gender equality. These notions seem reasonable and worthy of support. So why has so much of the public resisted or ridiculed the social justice warrior? The answer lies in extremism. The fringes of the social justice movement are so loud, so hyperbolic, so divisive, and often so tragically wrongheaded that they have managed to brand onto the public consciousness a twisted caricature of reasonable social justice. The extreme SJWs have totally lost the plot.

It was April 2018. Eighteen-year-old Keziah Daum wore a Chinese-style dress—a *qipao*—to her high school prom and posted the photos online.

The qipao is a form-fitting, slit-skirted dress developed in Shanghai and popularized among Chinese socialites throughout the twentieth century. Almost immediately a Twitter user responded angrily.

 Bôh

My culture is NOT your goddamn prom dress.

The Internet exploded. Bôh's outburst was retweeted nearly 42,000 times. The claim was that Daum had disrespected Asians in a callous act of "cultural appropriation." Chinese apparel belonged to Chinese culture, and Daum had disrespected and exploited that culture. In a follow-up tweet, Bôh said Keziah's wearing of the dress was "parallel to colonial ideology." Social media pages devolved into shouting matches. The indignant ranted about privilege and snowflakes. The controversy was so intense that it was covered in major media outlets like *USA Today* and CNN.

The interesting thing? When this story soon reached Asia, most people in mainland China, Hong Kong, and Taiwan were completely unbothered. Some were quite complimentary and happy to have Chinese culture represented on the other side of the world, as a Hong Kong commentator told the New York Times, "From the perspective of a Chinese person, if a foreign woman wears a qipao and thinks she looks pretty, then why shouldn't she wear it?"[340] Keziah herself agreed.

 Keziah ⊘   Apr 28, 2018
Replying to
To everyone causing so much negativity: I mean no disrespect to the Chinese culture. I'm simply showing my appreciation to their culture. I'm not deleting my post because I've done nothing but show my love for the culture. It's a fucking dress. And it's beautiful.

---

340 The New York Times "Teenager's Prom Dress Stirs Furor in U.S.—but Not in China" May 2, 2018

Keziah is absolutely correct. It's a fucking dress. And it's beautiful.

Some vocal liberals wail about "offenses" like these—offenses that don't exist—and their misplaced outrage plays right into the hands of conservative pundits such as Bill O'Reilly, a man who *aches* for an opportunity to lampoon *all* lefties as snowflakes and crybabies. Fox News often posts articles about "The Loony Left," and extremists jump directly in front of those accusations.

I'm not validating the conservative canard that liberalism breeds a snowflake mentality. Especially in the online age, there are kneejerkers on all sides, but I am admitting that some on the Left ignore the bona fide tempest because they're distracted by the teacup, wasting valuable time and energy that could and should be directed at other, more worthy issues. Many are binary thinkers. Their choices are A or B, yes or no, wonderful or horrible. There is no middle ground. As a result, there is no empathy or charity.

Offense archaeologists dig up a decade-old homophobic tweet by comedian Kevin Hart, resulting in his dismissal as 2019 host of the Academy Awards. Protesters demand that actor Liam Neeson be digitally removed from the film *Men in Black 4* because he admitted to hateful, racist ideas in his youth. MAGA-hat-wearing Covington High School student Nick Sandmann receives an avalanche of hate because he smirked at a rally and is gifted the opportunity to cash in with defamation lawsuits.

I have some amusing personal examples. In a recent online conversation about history's tyrants, I made a reference to "Hitler the madman." My interlocutor immediately chastised me for being ableist, aligning the genocidal dictator with everyday people who suffer from mental illness. That Twitter thread went on for days. In a similar exchange, I lamented the misspent energy of those constantly primed to feel *hysterical*. I was condemned as a misogynist for using a term that roots to an ancient claim—by men—that women were inferior and prone to emotional hysterics. Of course, I was using the colloquial version of "hysterical," but my challenger was eager to align me with the oppressive male authority of the Medieval period.

Complicating the problem is the reality that manufactured outrage is a strategy for malcontents and trolls craving attention and disruption, and then there are the Internet bots purposefully designed to foster online conflict for clicks, which generates ad revenue. The more people mash at their angry keyboards, the more money opportunists make.

Liberals should—we must—acknowledge the misplaced militancy within our own camp, because it's important to keep our ship seaworthy, and because we don't want to surrender these criticisms to opponents eager to paint all progressives with an extremist brush. Nothing will stop the Fox Newsers from taunting liberal "snowflakes" (as seen with the laughably dishonest Trump website snowflakevictory.com), but we can make strong, important, humanist ideas more difficult to misrepresent. This effort requires thoughtfulness and consideration and, crucially, education on key progressive subjects. After all, many objects of conservative ridicule aren't just liberal notions; they're the kind, considerate, humanist thing to do.

Trigger warnings warn of potentially disturbing content. Right-wing media shouts, "Suck it up, snowflake!" with little regard for the reality that society uses content warnings every day. Isn't it perfectly reasonable to tell a viewer, listener, or reader, "This film/show/book/speech includes some heavy stuff?" Isn't it an act of compassion to warn potential sufferers of sexual trauma about depictions of rape or violent sexual imagery, or warn PTSD sufferers about violent war footage, or prepare general audiences for a deeply disturbing and shocking film, as it does with the commonly accepted ratings system? (Personally I prefer the term "content warning" over "trigger warning," because the public seems to have a better understanding of the former and it lacks the cultural baggage.)

Note that I'm not absolving the public from responsibility. The ticket buyer complaining about a provocative comedian has admittedly cried "danger" after stepping in front of the bullet, but there is merit in packaging provocative content to prevent unnecessary harm to the genuinely wounded. This seems reasonable.

Safe spaces are places where (often marginalized) people can gather without fear of judgment or being ostracized. The idea is simply, "Come on in. You can be yourself here. It's a safe space." Many scoff at the idea, which seems a tremendously callous attitude toward people who have been isolated or mistreated because of race, religion, gender, trauma, disability, and more.

There are legitimate concerns about safe spaces. Greg Lukianoff and Jonathan Haidt wrote the 2018 book *The Coddling of the American Mind,* and they make some salient points about a frequently over-sensitive culture of helicopter parents, perpetually affected youth unequipped for life's hard realities, and intolerant of controversial ideas on school campuses. I'm reminded of the blowup at Middlebury College on March 2, 2017, when controversial speaker Charles Murray was scheduled for a discussion with political scientist Professor Allison Stanger. As Murray began, student protesters erupted in shouts, heckling, and even violent behavior so toxic that the university issued a public apology and disciplined the worst student offenders.

Even those in opposition to Murray's invitation could have disagreed in a way that didn't devolve into tantrums and chaos (like faculty members who went on record with a formal protest letter), but the student shout-down reflects the progressive fringe I've been referring to. Personally, I lament that an arena designed for the vetting of ideas became a No Speech Zone, and I would like to have seen Professor Stanger hyper-focus her intellect and expertise on Murray's claims. There would have been light, and there would also have been heat, and the audience members would have had the opportunity to witness a constructive vetting of ideas under that white-hot beam.

I'm certainly not opposed to "safe spaces" in a narrow context, but it's important that we prime our attitudes so that we can encounter and engage with different people and opinions, even when those people and opinions are terribly wrong. And to a great degree, it is our responsibility to stop gifting other people the power to drive us over a cliff. There are many offensive things in this world, but so often, offense is taken more than given, and we each have a personal responsibility to manage the buttons this world is so eager to push.

Political correctness is a common conversation-stopping term that is often used to defend the marginalization of minorities and justify bigotry and bad ideas. Many conservatives resistant to any form of social change wince at PC culture as an attack on traditional values.

Anti-PC attitudes, however, betray the notion that people have never had misguided ideas, and they often reveal a callousness about other people. Declare that it's more inclusive to say "humankind" instead of "mankind," and critics huff. Insist that "retard" is a cruel and distasteful slur against mentally disabled people, and critics jeer. Suggest replacing the racially problematic "Redskins" with a less loaded NFL team name that doesn't invoke white oppression of Native Americans, and critics scorn. Applaud the removal of monuments celebrating Civil War racists, and critics wail that America is betraying its heritage. Establish anti-bullying school programs to foster respect and protect children, and critics cry, "Just tell your kid to toughen up."

I'd argue that the above examples don't reflect what is politically correct. They represent what is technically correct, even morally correct. They are simply kinder, fairer, and more humanistic approaches to the issues.

On cue, the progressive fringes will take those meritorious notions about acceptance and kindness and push them into caricature. They speak of micro-aggressions and claim that audience clapping might be an act of exclusion among students averse to noise. They lambast legitimate concerns about the health problems of obesity with cries of "fat shaming." (Fat shaming exists, but not in the context of health analysis.) They declare it problematic to talk about male masculinity or female femininity, as those things promote gender stereotypes. They say that calling something "lame" is disrespectful to everyone with injured limbs. And we've already addressed the misplaced outrage over cultural appropriation.

As difficult as it is for some of my fellow liberals to accept, there exists a coddled sect of hypersensitive and overly dramatic people who navigate the world in a perpetually offended state, and I feel it's dishonest to ignore that reality. It's also critical that liberals resist extremism, a phenomenon that exists in almost every tribe: familial, political, religious, or ideological. We can be anti-fascism while condemning Antifa. We can be satirical and mocking without being base and vile. We can display fierce opposition without throwing milkshakes or fists at those we oppose. We can be defiant without being lawless. And we must clean up our own liberal house before it is burned to the ground by arsonists.

I'm exhausted at the purity tests imposed by extreme liberal factions infatuated with disqualifiers. *White people can't speak to racial issues. Men can't support feminist causes. Straight people shouldn't attempt LGBT advocacy. Westerners can't analyze or criticize non-Western attitudes, especially regarding Islam.* At the risk of offending the woke with "ableist" language, this is insanity. While it's true that our specific experiences are often shaped by color and culture, we can all relate to common denominators within the human experience (like confusion, rejection, pain, curiosity, joy, love, and connection), and we can rally to support people beyond ourselves instead of sequestering into intolerant cults of exclusivity.

Even now, the extremists are aghast at my insensitivity, discounting me as the product of white male privilege instead of a humanist ally. Their protestations prove my point about intolerance, purity tests, and binary thinking, and they reveal an "assume the worst" tendency to declare war on those who express even the slightest disagreement. We may align 95 percent on important issues, but the remaining 5 percent cannot be abided. This is a legitimate problem, and it needs to be rectified if we're going to affect positive change. Let the right-wing outrage machine drown in irony as it calls liberals "snowflakes" while frothing about inclusion, the secular Constitution, and non-existent emergencies like the "War on Christmas." We expect them to get it wrong. Within our own camp, we can do better.

I wrote this book because I'm desperate to see this world embrace positive change. As I emerged from my religious and political co-coons, I discovered positive change happening within myself, and it was indescribably freeing. I was able to discard my unwarranted fears about the Other. I was emboldened to pursue knowledge beyond the edicts of an anonymously written holy book. I was able to release my misplaced anger over imaginary threats to focus my energies on legitimate problems. And I discovered the joys of looking beyond myself into the wide, wild spectrum of humanity to appreciate people, ideas, and experiences I had never previously known.

If given the opportunity, I'd never go back into my Fox News bubble, the narrow church halls, radio rants, Tea Party rallies, and the daily prime time outrage. That environment wasn't the haven it claimed to be. It was a fear culture casting off large swaths of good people, good ideas, and goodness. It was more interested in lowering others than raising itself. It was constantly dividing humanity: Christian versus non-Christian, Republican versus Democrat, white versus non-white, straight versus non-straight, domestic versus foreigner, good versus evil. And it preyed upon human ignorance and insecurity to consolidate privilege and power.

There will always be those who take comfort in being told who they are, what they think, and what to do, and they'll likely continue to follow whatever Authority fits their inherited or otherwise established opinions. They'll cling to their god and shout about the Devil. They'll perch on their mountains and look down upon the unwashed. They'll build up their walls and load their firearms. And they'll remain strangers to those who don't look like them, talk like them, or think like them. What a tragic thing!

I have no illusions that any party or platform is perfect. I'm an imperfect liberal. I belong to an imperfect Democratic Party. I'm a member of imperfect humanity. But I have examined this world through the lens of a humanist value system, and I remain convinced that the liberal position is most aligned with constitutional religious liberty, equality for all, and the critical mission to alleviate suffering on all sides of our subjectively drawn borders.

I'm not a humanist because I am a liberal. I am a liberal because I'm a humanist.

If you take issue with liberals or with me, I respect your right to hold that position, and I hope that this journey into the darker corners of evangelical conservatism prompts a moment of reflection and consideration. Ultimately, because *mainstream* liberals are not the snowflakes that Fox News so often lampoons, we can exist in the same space, exchange disagreeing ideas with charity, challenge each other and ourselves, and operate in good faith to see the best ideas win the day.

If those ideas make us uncomfortable, perhaps that is a good place to start. As Oscar Wilde famously said: "An idea that is not dangerous is unworthy of being called an idea at all."[341]

---

341 The Epigrams of Oscar Wilde, edited by Alvin Redman (1954)

Learn more about Seth Andrews, his broadcasts, and his books at
SethAndrews.com